TEN: POETS OF THE NEW GENERATION

Also available from Bloodaxe

Ten: new poets from Spread the Word (2010)
Edited by Bernardine Evaristo and Daljit Nagra
Includes Mir Mahfuz Ali, Rowyda Amin, Malika Booker, Roger Robinson, Karen McCarthy Woolf, Nick Makoha, Denise Saul, Seni Seneviratne, Shazea Quraishi and Janet Kofi-Tsekpo.

Ten: the new wave (2014)
Edited by Karen McCarthy Woolf
Includes Mona Arshi, Jay Bernard, Kayo Chingonyi, Rishi Dastidar, Edward Doegar, Inua Ellams, Sarah Howe, Adam Lowe, Eileen Pun and Warsan Shire.

TEN

POETS OF THE
NEW GENERATION

EDITED BY
KAREN McCARTHY WOOLF

THE COMPLETE WORKS III

BLOODAXE BOOKS

ISBN: 978 1 78037 382 9

First published 2017 by
The Complete Works
in association with
Bloodaxe Books Ltd,
Eastburn,
South Park,
Hexham,
Northumberland NE46 1BS.

www.bloodaxebooks.com
For further information about Bloodaxe titles
please visit our website or write to
the above address for a catalogue.

Supported using public funding by
**ARTS COUNCIL
ENGLAND**

Printed in Great Britain by Bell & Bain Limited, Glasgow, Scotland, on
acid-free paper sourced from mills with FSC chain of custody certification.

CONTENTS

11   NATHALIE TEITLER: *Preface*

13   KAREN McCARTHY WOOLF: *Introduction:*
       A Beautiful and Necessary Complexity

1 ■ OMIKEMI NATACHA BRYAN

21   *Comment:* PASCALE PETIT

23   While She Waits for a Heart to Arrive
25   Crownsville
27   Queen
29   Salt
30   The Warner
33   You know I'd love you if I had a heart

2 ■ VICTORIA ADUKWEI BULLEY

38   *Comment:* CATHERINE SMITH

40   About Ana
41   Girls in Arpeggio
44   Lost Belonging
45   Retreat
47   Why can't a K be beautiful and magick?

3 ■ WILL HARRIS

51   *Comment:* SARAH HOWE

54   Object
55   Mother's Country
56   Halo 2
57   Self-portrait in front of a small mirror
58   Bee Glue
59   Diyarbakır

4 ■ IAN HUMPHREYS

63   *Comment:* MONA ARSHI

65   Zebra on East 55th and 3rd
66   The Man in the Rah-Rah Skirt
68   *London, 1997; Hong Kong, 1995*
69   The Mind Gap
71   Dragged Under
73   Skye and Sea

5 ■ MOMTAZA MEHRI

76   *Comment:* PASCALE PETIT

78   I believe in the transformative power of cocoa butter
     and breakfast cereal in the afternoon
80   Dis-rupture
82   <p>Grief in HTML</p>
83   The unthought has a comb
85   Asmara Road, NW2

6 ■ DEGNA STONE

88   *Comment:* LIZ BERRY

90   Swimming
91   *from* A Lick of Me Shoe
94   Mr Stone's Bionic Heart
95   The River Gods
96   Crossbones Burial Ground

7 ■ YOMI SODE

99   *Comment:* W.N. HERBERT

101   The Exhibition
103   Wón Ti Dé
104   The Outing
105   Night Terrors
106   The Man Behind the Switch
107   Distant Daily *Ijó*
110   After life

8 ■ JENNIFER LEE TSAI

113   *Comment:* KAREN McCARTHY WOOLF

115   New Territories
118   Parkgate
120   The Valley Spirit Never Dies
121   Black Star
122   A Certain Purity of Light
124   Going Home
126   Doppelgänger

9 ■ RAYMOND ANTROBUS

129   *Comment:* HANNAH LOWE
131   To Sweeten Bitter
133   Echo
136   Jamaican British

10 ■ LEONARDO BOIX

139   *Comment:* MICHAEL SCHMIDT

141   Pigments *alla prima*
144   Ode to Deal (Oda a Deal)
151   The Last Judgement (Bosch Triptych)

153   *Editor's biography*
154   *Mentor biographies*
159   *Acknowledgements*

PREFACE

Founded by writer Bernardine Evaristo, MBE, The Complete Works (TCW) has always had a specific, purpose: to counter the dismal lack of black and Asian poets published by major presses – less than 1% in 2007.[1]

At the time of its formation in 2008, there was no way of knowing if it would succeed: could the landscape of British poetry be shifted by just one initiative? An initiative that had at its heart not a major advocacy programme, but rather the development of exceptionally talented individual poets, ten per round?

The answer, as it turned out, was an unequivocal 'yes'. Now in its third round, there is no doubt that the programme has exceeded all expectations to become one of the most successful diversity programmes in the history of British arts. BAME poets now make up between 12-14% of those published by major presses, a phenomenal shift.[2]

And it's not just about the numbers. Two poets from the previous round of The Complete Works, Sarah Howe and Mona Arshi, have won the T.S. Eliot and Forward First Collection Prize respectively. Warsan Shire became a household name after her poetry was used by Beyoncé throughout the million-selling album *Lemonade*. Other TCW poets have been busy judging some of the world's most significant poetry competitions and editing key journals and reviews. A further eight new collections are due to be published through 2017. All of this makes TCW an international leader as a poetry collective.

The poets in this anthology – the third in the series published by Bloodaxe – offer an exciting new chapter in the history of the The Complete Works. Its diversity continues to grow and become more complex: we have the first Anglo-Latino poet, the first hard of hearing poet and a significant LGBT presence. And poetry is found in everything from ancient myths to Grime, all framed with an unmistakably British accent. As editor Karen McCarthy Woolf notes, this is poetry in which diversity is synonymous with complexity – it is poetry which demonstrates that the more we delve into diversity, the more we will find that each individual is unique.

And it is within this uniqueness that we are most likely to find similarities: not just through race and cultural affinities but because of the passions, obsessions and individual quirks which make each of us who we are. At a time when many of us find ourselves living in a 'post-truth' political landscape, the most important thing we can do as artists or activists is to build bridges not walls.

And as the Complete Works poets have shown, by developing the unique voice of each exceptional individual we can change the paradigm of the poetry world – and the wider world too. We can show that diversity and quality are synonymous, that art does have the power to change people and the societies they live in, and to offer us new ways of communicating – being, even.

■ NATHALIE TEITLER

1. The *Free Verse* report into diversity in UK poetry was published in 2007 by Arts Council England in association with writer development organisation Spread the Word.

2. Estimated; more detailed figures to be found in the updated version of *Free Verse*, published in autumn 2017.

INTRODUCTION

A Beautiful and Necessary Complexity

The Complete Works exists in order to increase diversity in British poetry publishing. This, the third wave of ten poets, selected nationally from regions across the UK, is further, irrefutable testament to the success of that intention. In various and contrasting ways, the poets herein challenge the paradigm of identity as a political, historical and literary phenomenon. Their geographies are wide ranging: amongst the group all five continents are represented and consequently so too, moments of linguistic and cultural hyphenation and hybridity. The work is passionate, urgent; sometimes intricate, at others powerful in its simplicity and tenor. In one way or another, each poet pushes at the limitations of the binary, whether through form or content, absence or exposure. Adrian Mitchell famously wrote that 'most people ignore most poetry because most poetry ignores most people': the poets in *Ten: poets of the new generation* do the opposite. Not by writing work that becomes meaningless as polemic or stereotype, for these are the pitfalls of politically alert material, but by creating poems with a reach and ambition that stretches out-wards towards the reader, with the skill and dexterity required to embrace the pressing complexities that this second decade of the 21st century presents.

And the notion of who that reader might be is also ampli-fied through allusion and influence, from Whitney Houston to the Anglo-Saxon warrior queen Æthelflæd, from Mahmoud Darwish to Li Po, from Grime to what Momtaza Mehri describes as a belief in the 'transformative power of cocoa butter and breakfast cereal in the afternoon'.

Mona Arshi, mentor to Ian Humphreys, reports that Ian uses the term '*offcumden*' a Yorkshire dialect word that translates as 'outsider' when discussing his poetics. Yet, there is a transformative and mesmeric quality to his writing that draws the reader centre-stage – not to the Hughesian moor that one might expect of his locale, but rather to a breezy and irresistibly meandering contemplation of 'The Man in the Rah-Rah Skirt', as if an African-European-Latin/American-Asian version of Frank O'Hara had suddenly rocked up at the 592 bus stop in Halifax. This ability to surprise, in terms of tone and approach, is a communal feature of the anthology. These are poets, not only willing, but also at their most comfortable when expressing multiplicities, often situating themselves not at the margins of an establishment to which they have no access, but at the centre of their own, self-divined universe, at the touchpoint of the inbetween. At times that touchpoint is necessarily terse in its confrontations, as in Raymond Antrobus's stark yet affecting account of growing up 'Jamaican British', where cousins in Kingston called him 'Jah-English' or Will Harris's tightly wrought 'Object' – a tautological consideration of the self as (non)binary construct. Antrobus explores his own experience of deafness, in a sequence, 'Echo' – and again the modalities of absence and presence play out, this time via sensory rather than cultural dimensions.

The body is also a significant literary site and occasion, as an expression of both womanhood and masculinity. Victoria Adukwei Bulley's 'About Ana' recalls the Cuban-American artist Ana Mendieta, who fell, mysteriously (and somewhat paradoxically considering the body was very much her canvas) to her death from a New York high rise. In its conclusion

Bulley declares that she is 'bored with fig leaves/and shames I did not choose' – intimating a characteristic rejection and simultaneous transformation of societal strictures. This glance towards religiosity is mirrored in the work of Omikemi Natacha Bryan, whose research into mourning rituals such as the Caribbean 'nine nights' coupled with a continuing practice in Angolan Capoeira, plays out subtextually in poems that capture both the heart and the mind through a linguistic palette heightened by the drama and lyric intensities of English-Jamaican hybrid rhythms and vocabulary. Ritual of another, more contemporary kind, also occupies a space at the centre of Yomi Sode's ethically attentive and musically capacious poetry and poetics. Black masculinity falls under the spotlight in a tender yet questioning exploration of fatherhood in 'Night Terrors', as do the legacies of institutionalised racism, street violence and their attendant impacts on mental health, while 'The Exhibition' probes at the hypocrisies lurking within the discourses of race and gender.

Elsewhere, the landscape of the body gives way to the actual environment and its human as well as spirit occupants. Degna Stone's 'A Lick of Me Shoe' is excerpted from a longer sequence that seeks to give voice and historicity to a working-class girlhood of the West Midlands – an ambition and trajectory that makes the mentor-poet pairing with Liz Berry ideal. Home and its co-ordinates, whether local, stratospheric or diasporic is also a preoccupation for Jennifer Lee Tsai, who explores her Chinese-Liverpudlian roots in poems that seek to understand 'New Territories' of loss and belonging in their relationship with ancestors, family, lovers, literature and locale. Leonardo Boix's achingly beautiful long poem 'Ode to Deal' is also concerned with geographies and diaspora, proximity and distance: between the different places and particularities we circumscribe as home, whether it is South

America or the UK, between lovers, or between the horizon as it meets the sea. Here, he effortlessly juxtaposes the fleeting quality of the watercolour and a sharp eye for quotidian and botanical detail with a languorous contemplation of sexual and sensual desire, where 'home' is both a sub-tropical garden populated by hostas and African soapberry plants and 'the protection of our English bed'.

Momtaza Mehri's urgent and dynamic poems are perhaps most iconic to the anthology at large. Her mentor Pascale Petit identifies a 'surreal gravity' of approach and there is an electric tension between the pressures of politics, inequality and societal upheaval and the desire to make a poetry that might somehow diffuse the pain of waking in a world that is 'romantically invested / in splitting me apart', a place where 'Death is an ellipsis' ('<p>Grief in HTML</p>'). Formally, Mehri allows the line to drive these extraordinary and vigorous energies towards a restorative, redemptive conclusion, where the poet (and thus the reader) can 'believe in a place where we can be ugly and poor and needy and still wear crowns'.

Poetry has always acknowledged its surroundings, even if obliquely: Romanticism was a poetry of witness in its response to the industrial revolution, Modernism reflected a wider impulse for change in society as the 20th century turned and rumbled into world war. Now the situation we find ourselves in collectively is one where the extremities of global politics, ecological and economic instability and violent conflict are creating a climate of apprehension and uncertainty. Whether it is a conscious or a subliminal act the ambience and archi-tectures of contemporary poetry are observant of these environmental conditions. Poets with hybrid sensibilities are becoming part of the mainstream and there is opportunity in the multifarious capacities that technology and its platforms bring to the ways in which we read and receive narrative, whether it is on a stage, screen, piece of paper or as a linguistic or grammatical intervention. For the next generation of poets, the challenge will be to incorporate these complexities in a manner that leaves scope for awe and wonder as well as elegy and critique. Writers of colour and diversity have long been grappling with the need, whether externally or self-imposed, to negotiate and process an experience of 'othering': embracing complexity is therefore a natural and practised response and one that the poets in this anthology take on with gusto and élan.

■ KAREN McCARTHY WOOLF

OMIKEMI NATACHA BRYAN

■ **OMIKEMI NATACHA BRYAN** is a poet and performance maker. She grew up in south London with her Jamaican grandparents. Her work has been published in numerous magazines including *Iota*, *Ambit* and *The Rialto*. Her debut pamphlet poetry collection, *If I talked everything my eyes saw*, won the 2014 Pighog/ Poetry School pamphlet competition. Ritual plays an important role in her arts practice, which also includes movement practices such as Capoeira Angola and visual art. Her ritual theatre performance, *Nine Night*, was featured as part of The Yard's 2015 experimental theatre festival. ■

■ PASCALE PETIT:

Omikemi Natacha Bryan's poems are spellbinding incantations to transmute trauma. Violent things happen: a girl is found assaulted on the bank of a a stream, a drug addict plugs himself into an electric socket, a mother is run over by a truck, a chest is plundered for a heart, and a god is summoned to help, but 'God / was on his knees / swallowing a pitchfork in an alley'. Ordeals are transformed through conjuring tricks mainly achieved through the electrifying vigour of her lines. Bryan has a knack for adroit effects, but it isn't just the images that slide about and melt into each other, the rhythm syncopates like improvised jazz, or the Capoeira Angola that she practises.

Chants – sometimes in dialect – help to create a heightened atmosphere, where what's going on evades logic, moves with an intensity that speaks to our subconscious, as if something indescribable is being articulated on a subliminal level. There is the sense of an unspeakable story ghosting the articulated lyric, a truth that dares not be written.

Often the subject animating the poems is an ancestral character, such as the Warner, or charismatic *Queen*, or a guileless child. These characters speak in riddles or behave like ecstatics, but it is because of the dynamic propulsion of The lines that they enthral us and can perform their lifesaving spells:

> *Queen* stand up before me
>
> sparkle and shine like the sun dancing in spider's silk
> then flickered and swayed until she melt, come like a pool in the
>   earth.
> At that time my head turned east, the rest of me stayed west
> while her body of water spread till I was standing in her dress.

What is compelling about such portraits is how images and people blend into one another, in a sleight of hand where matter can shape-shift in a blink. Birds, feathers and whirlwinds sweep through and come to the narrator's rescue. Such pyrotechnics give the poems a breathless pace. But it's the simple descriptions that astonish, similes such as: 'The people's mouths hung like udders,' and a girl 'laid there / like an instrument, waiting to be played'.

Bryan's influences include the disturbing but hopeful writing of Sapphire, Anthony Joseph's autobiographical sequences, most notably *Bird Head Son*, and writer-activist Toni Cade Bambara. Like Bambara, Bryan excavates forgotten histories. In her poem 'Crownsville' – a hospital formerly known as The Home for the Negro Insane, where children were subjected to unethical medical experiments – two children, Elsie Lacks and a ghostly boy, enact a ritual to escape their dire circumstances. They swim across the floor and escape, 'using the chain from the sink we'd be there in no time'. Such moments of magical realism are rendered even more effective by these rudimentary props, and this, together with a mesmerising musicality, offers us the possibility of divine redemption, which is of course poetry, where 'the door is a wing on a thread'. ■

While She Waits for a Heart to Arrive
(a Prayer)

In a backroom
where stories & names
are exchanged
& forgotten
in the same breath
I begin to speak
a truth that burns   falls apart
in my mouth –
ash & dust   that cannot
be put back together
as God
put us together   mother
& daughter

This evening
I pray for rainfall
the way gravel
can be raised into a mountain,
while my mother waits
for the traffic lights to change
I pray for rain
to slick the wheels
wheels that do not

       stop

my mother's eyes –
a handbag spilled
in the street   lips

rolling back
& forth in a tube

The light was red
but the driver kept going

     stop

she said

      stop

I said
but he kept going

& the brother
on the bottom bunk
heard nothing
& my mother
turned over
& the lights out

There were no eyes
so the lights were green
& God
was on his knees
swallowing a pitchfork in an alley.

Crownsville

Crownsville is a hospital in Maryland, United States, formerly
known as the Home for the Negro Insane. Many unethical
medical experiments took place at the hospital, particularly
on American-African children. One of the children was Elsie
Lacks, the daughter of Henrietta Lacks, who became known
for her 'immortal' cell line.

I prayed for Mattie, Hennie or anyone
who said they'd come but I haven't seen kin
since the last light we had was snow.
This week Joseph and Mary were having a baby
and getting buried, which is why we made caskets.
Nurse explained they were places for those
without beds to rest. Afternoons, I clawed dirt
until I found kin, climbed in   and laid there
like an instrument, waiting to be played.

~

Hennie said the mouth was the key of life.
I could call anytime, I didn't need wires, dials
not even lips to speak of light growing thin
and the room filling up with shadows
who will take me to Wilson – all I needed
was to close my eyes and like a sleight of hand
in a magic trick, she'd appear. But I think
she must be in the middle of something, maybe
one of those stories she'd tell me with the words
that suddenly get up   and leave.

~

When I close my eyes I see a porch light,
the door is a wing on a thread. Inside
there's a mat with gold and peppermint trim,
it's my space at the table, next to my sister, Mattie.
The trim frames a snowy scene; a black horse
and carriage, the rider is missing. Kin are waiting
for me before they start to eat but they know
I'm not grown enough to be heading home

                              on my own.

                              ~

Last night I woke to find Lucas in the bed next to me,
grinning, with three teeth and two empty caves in his face
I reached out to poke a finger in a hole,
but then he spoke, told me he could do anything,
like turning fallen leaves into sprinkles of dusk,
as he rubbed his hands into flames. Said
we could escape, play bandages instead of dead,
unravel like steam in our white sheets, that he
weren't made for the land but the sea and I for the sky,
as he took me on his back, we swam across the floor,
over bodies that tossed and rolled as we rode
and finally reached the window where he pointed
to the night, said the moon was an anchor we could climb,
using the chain from the sink we'd be there in no time.

Queen

She stood where you usually find the sun peeping over the
    ocean,
glowing in robes and a turban white like snow I'd never seen,
    except
when the foreign kin showed me in his story book. We had
    not seen light
since the boy's body was found dried up and gnarled like
    ginger root.

The parents had sent him for one of the remedies she made
    with the leaves,
to heal her legion as she liked to call them. Cousin Ramsey
    was one of them.
Suit doctors claimed he was cripple, told his parents he would
    have to learn
to walk on his belly like a lizard but *Queen* gave him back his
    legs

with two sticks from the bushes down by where she lived,
    the only house
in St Thomas to be painted red. Daddy would say is *Satan
    she working with.*
Mother being more scientific as she liked to call it, said it
    was because
the house used to belong to the sergeant till she stole his
    seed.

Built like a can of bully beef we'd fry up with onions at the
        end of the week,
her heels clicked when she passed through in those shoes;
        foreign credentials
she used to speak on all kinds of things, especially cud
that wasn't hers to chew. It was she, *Queen* stand up before me

sparkle and shine like the sun dancing in spider's silk
then flickered and swayed until she melt, come like a pool in
        the earth.
At that time my head turned east, the rest of me stayed west
while her body of water spread till I was standing in her dress.

Salt

Dixon stood listening to the water whistle and hiss till it sweet him like one of the Bailey girls from down the hill. Only a look but it was enough for the women to know they didn't want Dixon watching the children. The river had already snatched the tallest one everyone said favoured the Seven Keys man, *ca fe she lip heng like 'im n' red with 'im warnin'*, Mudda Ramsey would say but we were told to pay her no mind as her brain had taken in water. The girl was like a mountain peak with two carvings on her left cheek, a perch for Johncrow's landing each morning. Mainly it was the way she sang, so beautiful it felt like it was raining inside the church, when she was done a cool breeze would stroll through the room like a benediction. The Muddas knew her spirit was strong, it wasn't too long before one of them escorted her back to the chairs that half-way through the sermon acted more like a barricade for the Spirit. That's when I noticed Dixon running his hand up her leg and remembered that the Keys man said if I talked everything my eyes saw my mouth would tear. It was a Sunday when the stream hurried like little kin, bringing news of her tongue loose in her head, teeth gutted and her cream dress, lying torn on the water they say, *a salt it salt* like her.

The Warner

Stood and spoke in nothing
but the skin all of us were born in
with a mouth of hooks and mesh.
Cradled in the rim of her hat, eggs

and a mattress strapped to her back.
My eyes slipped in the dirt cracks.
Age of school, height of the Golden Stool
was I, when the bells called *doom doom.*

She roamed like a gully through highways
to preach inside the market place.
Her skin glowed like the night we had arrived –
sequins flitting on the cloak of night.

But this was daylight, Saturday afternoon
the sun swung low as a scythe moon.
It was unlike Parson's three-hour sermon
to repent and flee the *Everlasting Punishment.*

Men's lips are swollen by prayers and wishes
but their hands are crocheted from nets.
The great sharks we are in all out fishing
*   let us not forget.*

The voice was a muscular swell of wind
her words carried the smell of fish thawing.
Even the cows stood still like monuments
and stopped chewing their tongues to listen.

When they ask what manner of woman is this?
Tell them I am a mast in the midst of a tempest
a flame as fountain, a sail on a lantern
the dark artery in the hearts of men.

Her eyes looked as though she took a blade
scooped out the flesh to make two caves.
The people's mouths hung like udders.
Older brothers held onto their mothers.

Be humble as dust swept up by the wind
which is only the journey of time gathering.
Keep watch for a convocation of white coats,
ribbons of milt and feathers of smoke.

The Warner stopped, her hair a shock
a wish blown through a dandelion clock.
I kneeled to pick up one of the pins
as my head raised she began talking again:

Tell me who is your father?
I don't know him miss.

You is a little girl, every little girl has a father.
I don't know him miss.

Don't you want to know him?
I never thought it.

If you want to know follow, I will lead you to him.
But it's midday and the bell has been milked.

I only came to get flour.
For a little girl your tongue is sour.

Let me wet your hands with rum,
wash them, then give me your tongue
to drip honey on but don't swallow it
just wait for his spirit to come collect it.

My eyes caught red running down her thighs,
slow and sticky till the sap drew in flies
weaving in and out of her stride leaving behind
a coastline spread into a beach of light.

No miss, mother said I mustn't drink,
it's time to go, the bell already milk.

Then how will you know your father?
But is not I looking for him.

It was then bats flew from her tomb-like eyes,
she tilted her head and cast a net in the sky.

You know I'd love you if I had a heart

When love came more than 20,000 mouths were filled with
    candles & lined up in the streets.

~

You the first.   Inside   I build a church
                    a church with a child   inside
                                        a small child
inside   a church   inside her   a bird   a bird in her
                                        & a north wind
            growing sleepy in her head

~

You of the scars   of the scars   & would show without
                            anyone having to ask you
with the feelings   bingeing on them in the evening
                        washing them down with tears
            & siblings   siblings shouting   *she's just jealous*
                    & you
    putting the phone close enough so I could hear
                        you laughing through pony tears

~

You whowhowho   reminds me of thrush & running out of
    toothpaste
                            you of light rain
        & black-out blind of Sun's eye.
                    You rising up from the mud of sleep

with the dog teeth   you with the feathers & nails.
                                        You with the feathers
circling   you of the dowsing wind

                          ~

She was sad that love did not apologise at the inquest
          where doctors spent hours between her chest
                    & found no evidence of love being there.

                          ~

          You   irregular & hunched over   with bird
                              with dead bird   dead bird
you   with the silence   & voice buried under its engine.
                              You with the kinks
          of old telephone wires straightened out in conversations
                              you   collecting dust
               on my window sill   you who always leaves
                          without leaving

                          ~

          Certain kinds of love are hard to forget.

                          ~

You   who issued Love with a letter warning it would face a
     fine & court action if it continued.

                          ~

34

You at the wedding dancing to Whitney Houston
        captivating the camera man

                                                youwho
whowhowhowho is called a show off   you who learns how
        to tuck yourself in
                                        you with bird
        the dead bird in your throat   you with the feathers
                                with the mouth-watering menu
        who wants me to live out   the corner of your eye

                        ~

                        you with the bird
                                with the pony blues   mouth
rigged   with effects   loop pedalled   you with the feathers
with the feathers   you

VICTORIA ADUKWEI BULLEY

■ **VICTORIA ADUKWEI BULLEY** is a British-born Ghanaian poet and writer. A former member of the Barbican Young Poets, her work has been commissioned by the Royal Academy of Arts, in addition to being featured on BBC Radio 4. In 2016, she was shortlisted for the Brunel University International African Poetry Prize. Her debut pamphlet, *Girl B*, was released in the UK and US in 2017 as part of the African Poetry Book Fund's annual New Generation African Poets series, edited by Kwame Dawes. ■

■ CATHERINE SMITH:

Victoria Adukwei Bulley's bold, ambitious and questing poetry takes the reader on exhilarating and unpredictable journeys. As a British-born Ghanaian writer, she draws on a range of cultures, and her imagery opens up fresh possibilities for the reader. She delights in writing about *Language* – and *languages* – paying scrupulous attention to the nuances and possibilities of words – refusing to accept confinement; celebrating possibilities –

> Not all
> language is Romantic but all language is
> loved and lived through so

Her work can also be playful, engaging the reader with riddles and mysteries –

> But K is a creature
> unlike any else

Some of her boldest poems concern the body – her own, and those of others; the body as both private/ intimate, and public/political. Often, her unflinching gaze is directed at her younger self, opening up her own physical and emotional experiences of being a young black woman on the cusp of the exhilarating and de-stabilising journey of adolescence; her poems also project into imagined futures.

Her imagery is invigorating, often uncomfortable – 'a path stitched with nettles' darkens a dream – yet her poems are infused with a palpable compassion for the human condition, in all its messy contradictions. She has that rare ability in a poet – to be both inside and outside an experience; this makes reading her poetry stimulating and unsettling. She constructs ambitious, formally accomplished poems and is prepared to experiment, to take risks in terms of form and structure. This is a poet whose poetry is spiritual, personal and political; whose highly intelligent observations open up the reader's world.

> Don't touch her hair
> don't say her name, it has a K in it
> that don't belong to you.

About Ana

The truth is, nobody
        knows how Ana Mendieta
met her death. It would appear
        she was pushed. Some distance
below, the doorman said he heard
        a woman shout *No*, and then
the sound as her body
        hit the top of the diner
so hard her face left a mark
        like a postage stamp. In the photo
she is naked and feathered. She
        looks like the first woman,
like she doesn't know
        what a camera is, that somewhere
in the world it's believed
        these things can steal a soul.
Her arms are out, as if saying
        you move them like this, to fly.
Her feet are apart, you can see
        the circle of her hips,
the thicket between her legs.
        I look at her and think, this
is the true work of the body, this:
        to adorn itself and be
comfortable, unaware. I myself am
        bored by fig leaves
and shames I did not choose.

Girls in Arpeggio

1 *Early Intervention*

The smiles of the girls
on the children's relaxer kits
told no lies. They were too happy
to realise they were poster-girls
for the effacement of themselves.

Not knowing this either
we would sit there, still,
watching our mothers mix dreams
with a spatula; watching the mirror
from under the eaves
of our alkaline cream caps.
We stared at the girl on the box, willing
to be cleaned before sin,
and as the soft, pink science got working,
pleasantly tickling the skin, we waited
until our blood-borne bonds would break
just enough, perhaps,
for all in the world that resisted us
to straighten out.

2 *Forbearance*

There is a toll charged
for choosing to be the exotic one.
The problem has something to do

with your acceptance of a cage
made from laundered gold.

birds of paradise,
you were the first dreams to die
when the ships arrived / and when
they arrived / they belonged / and you
did not belong / unless
you belonged
to
them.

3 *Forgiveness*

Oh daughters of Eve,
did you know
you were a quarter-formed thing?
Or did you never pull the wings
off a fly, one by one, and wonder
what to name it then?

Or did they only tell you and tell you
walk tall; hold your heads high
you sweeter berries, you
picked-too-soon
and placed in the heat to dry
and stain the pavement
apologetically.

4 *Realpolitik*

Somewhere beyond the last of the pencil lines   tattooed
onto the doorframes of their kitchens   their only
nations   these girls, cacao-cored and peppercorn pin-
curled, decided to call themselves   beautiful.
Not   chocolate or caramel. Not coconut or tan. Not
Bounty, not Hovis best-of-both or burnt wholemeal toast.
Not Oreo or Coco Pops. Not buff nor carbon-cum-diamond
blick. Not lighty   not pick 'n' mix and match   not hair
enough to hang from. Not video girl. Not side chick. Not
thick. Not booty or apple-bottom. Not deputation any
longer, not another   word   not vice, not hereafter any
cover-teacher or stand-in nor prefix; no sign nor understudy,
no other   for *beauty*   any more.

For these girls it was a violent act.
But after it, they slept better.

Lost Belonging

I
left
my bag
on the train
under the table.
Forgot it, looking
at the sun as I rolled
home into the city. Gold
was spilling from the frame
of a skyscraper and it looked
like a fire but it was only nature
reflecting off of steel. It was nature,
at it again, refracting from the metals
of this skin that we have grown so lately.
Everything is going to break and I must get
home before it does, or doesn't yet, or buckles.
Back to the snug shut door, to the batteries +/ –
all dashed from the clock and the blinds closed tight,
a millipede of stinging eyes, red light crashing through
from the realm behind them. Mother. *Where else can I go?*

Retreat

4
Ruby says nothing.
Ruby cuts a tube of penne in half with the side of her fork,
a slow-motion blade stooping to kiss the back of my neck. A
warning. *Eat, before it gets cold; before you forget how to do it.*
Until now, I jigsawed her exposition to find the best fit.
Satisfied, I clean my plate.

3
I haven't seen a wasp in years, but there are *wasps* here,
larger than the ones I remember. Padma, our retreat leader,
climbs the bunk bed, removes a hornet from the room with
a cup.

2
Evan is a sixty-five year old retired father, just like Dad.
You remind me of my dad, I tell him, t*he only difference being,
of course, that you're white.*

4
Everybody has bought and is studying one of the many
dharma books on sale here, except Alastair, 84, who reads
Alistair Cooke, instead.

5
I am in the shrine room, closest to Buddha, when Evan is
crying. We two are the last ones left, but the room – vacant
– is loud with her, humming *Susan, Susan*, between each
caught breath.

1

The week begins when I turn off my phone. I delete the world as an infant does. I keep my palms flush over my eyes, until I realise I do not own a watch or an alarm clock.

8

Brother, may you be well. May you be happy. May you be free from suffering.

7

On the last evening, a sunset. My turn in the kitchen. Ruby offers to take my shift, so that I can walk with the others. It is the first time she's volunteered to speak to me, and when she calls me, I hear it like a song, and begin to love my name.

6

Barbara waves until my rearview mirror swings her face and wind-up hand out of sight. I will see her again, several times. I don't know this. Or, too, that she will even visit my house, sit with me on the floor of my parents' room, where it is quiet. Or that whenever I picture her, no matter how much in the future, she will always be waving goodbye.

Why can't a K be beautiful and magick?

It exists in knots but nobody will say
how it appeared there, why, who snitched
and stitched it up, or when.

It makes the shark's teeth cut as they do
when they slit enamel into bone easy
as plugs into coy sockets.

Does the K have a temper? Perhaps it should
because it sounds like a can't. Switch the a to
a u and it sounds like washing your mouth out with
Listerine –

this is a litany against the commonwealth of
anger displaced onto the K.
The K is not okay

the K is the most misunderstood, ignored, indentured
letter of all. But K is a creature
unlike any else. Insouciance magical.

What and why and where did it never exist
until now? Until *now*. Till before, where when Kemetic,
Kush, Khan, Kryptos, Knight, Afrika, Amerikkka – hey,
    bambaataa you

three Ks in a row that mean death. K where a C
used to be – watch me now – means a new life
existence evicted from exile into now

47

into the before-now,
don't ask how yet, but,
home again.

Not all pretty words end in Cs and easy-Es. Not all
language is Romantic but all language is
loved and lived through so

don't touch her hair
don't say her name, it has a K in it
that don't belong to you.

WILL HARRIS

■ **WILL HARRIS** was born in London, and is of Anglo-Indonesian heritage. He has worked in schools and as a tutor, co-edits the small press 13 Pages and organises *The Poetry Inquisition*, a night of poetry held to account. He co-edited *The Mimic Octopus*, an anthology of imitative verse celebrating the tentacular nature of poetic influence, and has run workshops on imitation and other aspects of craft at London's Southbank Centre. He has had work published in *The Poetry Review* and *The White Review*, among other places, and has been assistant editor of *The Rialto*. His debut pamphlet, *All this is implied*, is published by Happen*Stance*. ■

■ SARAH HOWE:

I first encountered Will Harris as the co-editor, with another young poet Richard Osmond, of an inventive journal series called *13 Pages*. Its editorial manifesto unashamedly celebrated 'craft and artifice – not in the sense of falseness, but rather a kind of irreducible, intricately well-made thoughtfulness'. As I came to know Will's own poems, I recognised in them that same quality: their 'thoughtfulness' apparent at a glance, but offering up new layers at each encounter. These are contemplative, mindful poems that pursue lines of argument or dramatise reflection, seeking out resonant images that will embody their questioning. But Will's poems are also 'thoughtful' in the sense that they are generous to their readers, reaching out a hand, heedful of our ability to follow however far they leap.

Craft and artifice are here in abundance, but are not deployed unthinkingly. Some of the poems make the ethics of artifice part of their own subject, as when 'Halo 2' watches a player roaming through the digital landscape of a games console Shoot 'Em Up, turning from the gore to linger over 'the birds singing in the artificial trees'. Alert readers might hear in their song Yeats's fable of the mechanical bird 'set upon a golden bough to sing' to a drowsy emperor. Such allusive moments are never superfluous, but turn a lens onto the very notion of literary tradition, highlighting the way these poems explore a tangled skein of inheritances, cultural, familial, linguistic and poetic. Will's skilled use of traditional forms is equally unobtrusive, often working just below the level of conscious registration. Sometimes I've gone back and realised a poem of his follows a strict rhyme scheme, where all I'd initially perceived had been an impression of music.

That music is present even in the most formally experimental of his poems. That ambitious strand of his work is represented here by a poem like 'Object', whose arrow-linked X and Y variables seem to press up against the limits of what can be put into language:

$X \rightarrow Y$ I have taken nothing from you.
$Y \rightarrow X$ Then I have taken nothing.

The poem sketches out a map of social bonds, power relations and lines of influence, which speak to the experience of an individual 'I' puzzling over what is handed down between generations, but also to the predicament of nations locked together by their colonial histories. The verb 'take', which resounds through the poem, might suggest plundering by Western imperial powers past and present. In the opposite direction, it might point to a mechanism like Homi Bhaba's theory of 'colonial mimicry', which describes how colonial subjects were compelled to 'take' their identity from their white oppressors, in adopting their manners and tongues. In *Black Skin, White Masks* (1952), Frantz Fanon wrote about how a black colonial subject like himself might grow up feeling psychically white, at least until the moment a white child pointed at him and cried 'Look, a Negro', prompting the tragic realisation of his denied personhood: 'I was an object in the midst of other objects.' Many of Will's poems are concerned with what it means to construct a self amidst the tortuous legacies of race, history and violence.

The poem 'Self-portrait in front of a small mirror' recounts a similar moment of racial interpellation, of *othering*, when 'a barman – standing in front of a row of spirits, endlessly mirrored – asks for my ID, refuses to accept my name as my own. *Will Harris?*' The pun on 'spirits' makes the well-stocked British bar morph fleetingly into a gallery of ancestors, in whom the poet sees his own face distortingly reflected. That poem's hall of mirrors is only the most overt instance of a broader theme, which emerges in poems full of reflections and uncanny doublings, adding up to a sense of identity as something less given and fixed than fluid and up-for-grabs.

One of the most exciting aspects of Will's work is the extent to which he draws on his mixed Indonesian, Chinese and English heritage to develop a poetics of mixed raceness – a topic still surprisingly unexplored in contemporary poetry. In her essay 'Speaking in Tongues', Zadie Smith described her aspirations for the then newly elected President Obama, a figure she saw (like herself) as being between races: 'It's my audacious hope that a man born and raised between opposing dogmas, between cultures, between voices, could not help but be aware of the extreme contingency of culture.' The work of Will Harris begins to feel its way towards a poetic shape for that audacious hope. ■

Mother's country

(Jakarta, 2009)

The shutters open for landing,
I see the pandan-leafed
interior expanding
towards the edge of a relieved
horizon. Down along
the banks of the Ciliwung
are slums I had forgotten,
the river like a loosely
sutured wound. As we begin
our descent into the black
smog of an emerging
power, I make out the tin
shacks, the stalls selling juices,
the red-tiled colonial
barracks, the new mall...
It is raining profusely.
After years of her urging
me to go, me holding back,
I have no more excuses.

Halo 2

There were those walls where brochure-like
paintings of a young Christ showed
his hairless body pricked with blood, aglow.
The artist, by a fine excess, had meant
to advertise his suffering. Late one night

playing *Halo 2* I saw myself in what
I saw on screen and, from Beaver Creek
to Uplift, shot anything that moved –
the birds singing in the artificial trees;
the true self nothing more than the self as seen.

Self-portrait in front of a small mirror

I pay close attention to the shape of my eyes, how my eyelids slope down towards the ridge of my nose – that fold of skin, which I will learn is the epicanthic fold, no more an indicator of race than my stubby little fingers or the mole at the centre of my chest. Just different. I am making a self-portrait in front of a small mirror propped up on my pencil case. How can I know that when I put aside the mirror, as I must, to encounter the world *with* and *through* those eyes, there will be questions: *where are you from? are you Korean? speak Chinese?* At seventeen, at Borders, I say my books are for an English degree and the man behind the counter grins, calls me a bright boy, and though it may be nothing – as he says it, I see myself reflected in the glossy wall display behind him – I feel accused. When I open my mouth in shops, though my voice will shrink into a weird RP, I will swallow the mantra of the colonial elite who, other in blood and colour but English in taste, spend their lives fulfilling Macaulay's dream of a state able to exert soft power by giving a pliable clique the illusion of self-rule. The illusion will remain intact long after I am presumed foreign, after a stranger tells me to *fuck off back home*, after a barman – standing in front of a row of spirits, endlessly mirrored – asks for my ID, refuses to accept my name as my own. *Will Harris?* My nasal bridge which, being lower-rooted, draws a fold of skin over the corners of my eyes, marks me out – as it does these words – for special treatment. But I must, and will, put aside the mirror.

Bee glue

I

'Break a vase,' says Derek Walcott, 'and the love
that reassembles the pieces will be stronger than
the love that took its symmetry for granted.'
When I read this I can only think *who broke it?*

In the British Museum, two black 'figures'
(they don't say slaves) beat olives from a tree;
a 'naked youth' stoops to gather the fallen
fruit. The freeborn men are elsewhere, safe

behind their porticos, arguing the world's
true form. They talk of bee glue, used
to seal the hive against attack, later called
propolis, meaning that it has to come
before – is crucial for – the making of a state.

II

Today it's summer and bees hum inside
the carcass of a split bin bag. A figure passes,
is close to past, when I see her face, half
shadow, glazed with sweat or tears, the folds

beneath each downcast eye the same
dark brown as, oceans off, my grandma. *Mak*.
I want a love that's unassimilated, sharp
as jagged shards of pots. That can't be taken,

granted. Think of Dad at work among
the fragments of a Ming vase – his job to get it
passable. He'd gather every piece and after
days assembling, filling in – putty, spit,
glue – draw forth not sweetness. Something new.

Diyarbakır

One day, a white rabbit read
my fortune, twitching as it chose

from several paper slips, soft head
straining at its harness, nose

scabbed, peeled back like bark.
Here, amid the desert, stark

as day, they tortured dissidents;
now paper slips blow between

the points of a barbed wire fence.
A life should not just be, but *mean*.

IAN HUMPHREYS

■ **IAN HUMPHREYS** was born in Bedfordshire, grew up in Cheshire, and has lived and worked in cities including Hong Kong, Sydney and London. Following a move to West Yorkshire, Ian began to write poetry and prose in 2013. His work has been published in magazines such as *Ambit*, *Poetry News* and *The Rialto*, as well as in anthologies in the UK and overseas. Ian won the 2016 Hamish Canham Prize and the PENfro Open Poetry Competition in 2013. His fiction has been shortlisted three times for the Bridport Prize. He holds an MA in Creative Writing (Poetry) from MMU's Manchester Writing School. ■

■ MONA ARSHI:

Ian Humphreys has only been writing poetry for five years but his poems have already been widely published and anthologised. What struck me when I first engaged with his poems were the dream-like angles from which he negotiates the world around him.

A natural poet, Ian has a highly individualist style; relaxed long lines with an instinct for allowing a poem to breath and speak before he discovers the poem for himself. As well as poise and fluency he has an enviable gift of finding final lines of poems many of which are seared on the surface of my memory.

There is something of the peculiar at work in Ian's poems in the way that is often used to describe Stevie Smith's work. His subjects and the way he translates the world around him in poetry are often familiar scenes, bus stops ('The Man in the Rah-Rah Skirt'), bathrooms ('Dragged Under') and tube rides ('The Mind Gap') but these never feel like safe homely enclosures. Instead with astonishing deftness he is able to latch onto an image or scenario and orbit around its circumference, reexamining, exploring and transforming what is there. Ian prefers the oblique glance but what's interesting to note is how often his poetry is steeped in the sense of the uncanny where the reader is un-settled by the grip of their childhood terrors. It's almost as if there is something of the 'aesthetics of the fearful' working beneath the surface of the poems. Ian's work is also lit with humour and wit; music and rhyme are also an important feature, which he allows to arise gently and employs with a lightness of touch.

Ian is of mixed heritage (Asian, European, African and Latin American) and he is now living in West Yorkshire. Ian uses the word '*Offcumden*' when discussing his poems. This is a Yorkshire dialect word meaning 'Outsider.' Ian and I discussed how far his hyphenated identity was tied up in writing 'strangerly' from the margins and how this may have filtered into his poetics.

These are generous poems from a skilful poet who is able to craft giddy-making revelatory lines but at the same time allows the reader to fully participate in experiencing them. ■

Zebra on East 55th and 3rd

Unfazed, he grazes on popcorn and nachos
from a *Keep New York City Clean* litter bin,
shrouded in a canopy of cloud that leaches
through the steel bars of a subway vent.

Sneakered commuters steam by, too busy
to notice, too drunk on mobile devices.
Outside P.J. Clarke's a woman's whistle
lassoes a yellow cab, hoists it kerbside.

Brooklyn, she snorts to the Iraqi driver.
The zebra lifts obsidian eyes, squints
at the transaction, the tap of a Yankees cap
and brays. His tail flicks sparks of iridescence

at the dark carcass of a neon sign advertising
 old Beer by a 24-hour liquor store. It lights up.
He trots to the pedestrian crossing,
waits for *walk* to burn white and vanishes.

The Man in the Rah-Rah Skirt

I'm waiting for the 592 at Halifax bus station
when I see a man in a rah-rah skirt and hiking boots
ahead of me in the queue. And I think,
why the rah-rah skirt? Didn't they go out
in the 1980s? Surely they're not back in fashion.
Will big hair and legwarmers follow?
Then it dawns on me how the skirt gets its name:
from the *rah! rah!* chants of cheerleaders
as they motivate (and titillate) teams of American jocks.
Perhaps that's why this man is wearing one.
He's signalling an allegiance to (or passion for)
the all-American male. Or female.
But why the big boots?
Are his feet too large for women's shoes?
It occurs to me the footwear may be a fashion statement.
The man may have opted for contrast
or simply an on-trend nonchalance.
I contemplate the style of skirt I'd choose
should I ever feel the urge to wear one.

I decide on a pencil skirt.
There's something about the way they sit demurely
below the knee, yet have a bondage edginess.
I picture the skirt forcing me to adopt a shuffling gait
like my great-grandmother circa 1910
in her mythic kimono, fluttering
through Bird Market in Mong Kok.
I find myself tugging at my jeans self-consciously,
smoothing out my elegant pencil skirt.
It mustn't ride up.
A man with a sleeve tattoo leans into me,
nods at the rah-rah skirt and says, *What the fuck is that?*
I cough a laugh.
Then I say, *It's a rah-rah skirt. They were big in the 1980s.*
The man grenades me a look, scratches his tattoo
(a mermaid playing what appears to be a ukulele).
He runs a coarse hand through muddy blond highlights.
Your hair looks old school George Michael, I almost say.
Instead, I pat down my jeans again.
Over by the bins, a pink-tinged pigeon
dances round the open purse of a samosa.

London, 1997; Hong Kong, 1995

Andy

When Andy wore his beat-up cowboy hat in the bath,
I knew he was heading out on the pull. In the bars,
he scowled at the crowd as if someone had whipped his drink.
Fat chance. He'd clutch his Jack Daniels and Coke tight all night
like a loaded pistol. He never went home alone.
Andy's cheekbones were blades. His put-downs sharper.
He smoked duty-free Marlboros. Or cadged mine.
After he died, I found out the umlaut on the 'o' of his surname
was his own invention. His favourite shirt – bone white
with an embroidered rose that crept across his chest like a scar.

Terran

He had a smile for everyone, even the doctors. We panicked
when he got sick. Too much anger and tequila, the impotence
of *why?* Someone made a concoction of rainforest fungi soup
that festered under his hospital bed for weeks. He drank it
secretly each morning, puked it back up before breakfast.
Dark magic felled him; maybe it could make him better.
At the crematorium in Kwai Chung, tongue-clicking attendants
in shorts and T-shirts flicked fag ash on the tiled floor.
They stared at the *gweilos*. We stared at Terran's coffin.
Flames rose Bunsen-burner blue through half-closed curtains.

The Mind Gap

A woman in a striped acrylic blouse
        perfume-bombs me as the packed train
to Paddington
                seals out St John's Wood.

She uncrumples a frown, straightens
        her newspaper. Then props it
carefully against
                the bridge of my nose.

'I think this lady may be attempting
        to dislodge my glasses,' I complain cheerily
to the man beside me.
                His face slides shut.

Contorting to escape the stink of ink,
        I become rapt by a tube ad that rattles on
about cut-rate
                Laser Eye Surgery.

The woman positions the skewer
        of a red court shoe on top of my
left unlaced brogue,
                applies pressure.

'Excuse me', I object into my iPhone.
        'I believe you're standing on my foot.'
'I'm so sorry,'
                she responds in Helvetica.

Then persists. 'I was just reading
            about you. It's such a tragedy…
your condition.'
                She lowers her mask.

The train is wolfed by the dank mouth
            of a tunnel. I can only see
her pumpkin grin.
                Firefly eyes.

I feel her heel pin me to the floor
            like a shadow. I make a stab at a scream
but all that escapes
                is an apology.

Dragged Under

So many wet shaves in a lifetime. How many thousands and
    thousands? So many

    rituals at dawn's bleached-bone altar, a falter of
    sharpened steel on skin.
So much water   feel it slide through your fingers.
  So many minutes turned to steam,
  clouding vision, sucked away into the city's mechanical lung.

        The roar and the rush

and, once in a while from nowhere, swirling in the vapours –
    the apparition of an old Cherokee myth.

        The Haunted Whirlpool

where warriors have been known to drown before breakfast.

Stare too long into its depths and you'll see a great company of
    men.

      Men who look a bit like you.   Ordinary men
    wearing their smartest suits, navy blue or funeral black.
      Grey-faced, blank-eyed, grumbling men.

      They beckon at you through the mist
  and eddies of foam.   'Come join us!' they cry,
        their teeth porcelain-white.

Watch how they slowly descend to hell
                                in a swell of red.
        How they frantically reach for you
                    before vanishing through the vortex.

        Sluiced into the guts of the megalopolis.

Later, glueing a poultice of toilet paper to your chin,
            you tell yourself   you're not like those men,

        those lost men, sunk and swallowed whole.

            And the face in the mirror
                            smiles in agreement
                    as he Double Windsors
                    Monday's tie – jerks it

                        snug.

Skye and Sea

A mist-washed bothy on the Isle of Skye
  where kestrels thread cloud to purple heather.
Breakfast is salted oats, a red kipper, sweet tea.
  There's just the one room, one chair, one spoon.

A snowed-in bothy on the Isle of Skye
  where ice slides a tongue under the door.
Ghost breath lingers like woodsmoke.
  Nights uncoil into Nosferatu shadows.

A sun-trawled bothy on the Isle of Skye
  with crow's nest views of otters on the loch.
Sheets draped, drying on a rowan tree.
  Wasps thieving kisses from the lip of a jar.

A whitewashed bothy, a kaleidoscope sky,
  where weather colours sea, mountain, mind.
Where the sole interference is a rush of tide
  over sand, tide over sand, time over sand.

MOMTAZA MEHRI

■ **MOMTAZA MEHRI** is a poet, essayist and co-editor of the digital platform Diaspora Drama. Her work is featured and forthcoming in *DAZED, Sukoon, Bone Bouquet, VINYL* and *Poetry International*. She has been shortlisted for the Brunel African Poetry Prize and the Plough Prize. Her chapbook *sugah.lump.prayer* will be published as part of the New Generation African Poets series, edited by Kwame Dawes and Chris Abani. With a background in biomedical science, she has worked as a health educator, translator and language teacher. She tries her best not to believe in astrology or borders. ■

■ PASCALE PETIT:

Momtaza Mehri is of East African heritage, and lives in London. She writes poems that are of urgent concern for us all in these turbulent times, and specifically address communities of the refugee diasporas. She draws from a broad spectrum of cultures and poetries from around the world, creating hybrids of high and low culture – the sheer range of her influences is impressive from someone still in her early twenties. These influences span the rich tradition of Somali poetry, including leading poet Faysal Mushteeg, classical Arabic ballads, Caribbean literatures, the Sudanese poet Muhammad al-Fayturi, Mahmoud Darwish, Essex Hemphill, slam poetry, old Egyptian cinema, and 90s Bollywood films.

As well as this polyphony that feeds her art, Momtaza's poems are notable for their engagement with cyberspace, and her training as a biomedical scientist gives her a forensic eye for detail when writing the body and the body politic. '<p>Grief in HTML</p>' encapsulates the fracturedness inherent in her poems, where hypertext codes are used to powerful effect to describe the aftermath of a bombing, where a monitor screen becomes the victim's crystal tomb, and her experiments with form in this poem, and in another titled 'Dis-rupture', which starts with a chilling, matter-of-fact list, enhance the sense of dislocation, plunging us into a merciless digital reality where Facebook is haunted by profiles of the dead, and where the collapse of the North Tower of the former World Trade Center reveals '100 boxes worth of the enslaved, their belongings'. Such poems expose grave truths about our era, are outward looking and hyperrealist in their surrealism.

This surreal gravity is typical of Momtaza's approach, as is her fusion of disparate elements – the intimate is juxtaposed with the public: a bomb wheezes like a child, a bridge is a film star's unibrow. But there is also a lightness of touch in throwaway phrases that celebrate survival as well as grieving, such as: 'and make a castle out of / this bottled sigh / they call living'. Even the titles of her poems, such as the one these lines are from – 'I believe in the transformative power of cocoa butter and breakfast cereal in the afternoon' – marry the joyful and tragic.

What binds Momtaza's complex art into a unified vision is her insight that tragedy is as ordinary as someone washing their hair. 'The unthought has a comb' is simultaneously a hair-wash and a semi-abstract painting of refugees drowning in waves. There may be no language to convey the horror but a comb can grip the scalp by its teeth, 'as the water swallows your people', and the narrator can 'loop a finger in coil and split / the shore in half'.

Sometimes this 'unthought' that pervades all her work cannot be conveyed in English, and Arabic comes to the rescue. While Momtaza does not wilfully obscure meaning, she will not sacrifice truth for a false clarity, her outlook is kaleidoscopic, reflecting an increasingly chaotic matrix. It's as if she is reconstructing language, re-appropriating it for nothing less than a quest for survival, and this hybridity of tongues, coupled with the bricolage of her indelible images, is a brave endeavour to mend the world. ■

I believe in the transformative power of cocoa butter and breakfast cereal in the afternoon.

Pick a sky and name it. The scriptures say there are seven.
We have enough time.
A fig, bruised-pink, resting on the dashboard,
tilted as if to say
'get it over with, khalaas'.

This breeze feels too much like an aunt, tugging at our scalps –
I think of how perfectly timed your buzzcut is.
How the border was dotted with goats,
lone whistle-blowers against concrete skyscrapers.
Here, in the country of your birth, we cross the Persian Gulf,
leaving a lush behind us. Here lies the stark of my bracelets,
green as Uganda.

A tunnel above us, reflected in a lucent drop of light on your
        cheek.
This liminal state between island and man.
Between Africa and The Peninsula,
the world's two thick thighs,
or heartbreaks.

Behind us, those we left behind still drink from time's cup,
under the same stars a prophet gazed up at.
They call them drones now. I think. Ahead,
I know even less,
except our feet hanging off a hotel bed;
a geologic upheaval.

Your mother sits in the glove compartment, the kohl shedding
    from her eyes.
I share you with her,
the way we share our unbelonging
and make a castle out of
this bottled sigh
they call living.

I believe in a place where we can be ugly and poor and needy
    and still wear crowns.

Take me there.

Dis-rupture

I

a) 20,000 bones sit below Lower Manhattan, under what was once known as a trade centre.

b) Under concrete pillars, you can find anything. Allegedly.

c) 40 percent of the bones belonged to children under twelve. All enslaved.

d) Property built above property.

e) 100 boxes worth of the enslaved, their belongings, were found in the North Tower, after its decennium crumple.

f) A bruised string. Archivists speculate. It could have been a slave's prayer beads, inscribed with His 99 names.

g) My grandmother rolls each stone between her fingers. She too counts backwards.

II

Tell me.

Was my mother's face a terror in the cockpit,
or a terror below it,
in the soup of mud and bitumen?

The skin of my elbows hangs loose as a murmur.
Sad girl litanies don't pay the bills,

or undo our architectures of longing. This, I know.
I wake daily to a world that is romantically invested
in splitting me apart.
Don't let me collude against myself.
Don't let me believe I am what I am not.

III

He tells me to change the channel. He's sick of watching
    bodies
that look like his own dying. Yaa rabb, it's a fucking looped
    record.
Puffs on a shisha pipe, apple fumes straddling the lounge,
a sweetness that takes nothing from us.
I flip to the satellite's distortion. A dubbed Bollywood
    picture,
Kajol's icon unibrow
stitching, then unstitching, into a bridge
big enough to take us somewhere
a little less red.

<p>**Grief in HTML**</p>

<p>The bomb explodes near the Central compound, makes a wheezing child-sound.</p>
<p>It's a Monday afternoon. A city sleeps on its side. Death is an ellipsis. Gasoline, cobalt, concrete, yarabbyarahmaan, a window shard clarifies itself against the slackness of suit and skin, imprints into the chest of a family friend. He is flesh made rupture. He is dressed in crystals. He is dissolved.</p>
<p>A father on the other side of a glass screen logs in. Facebook. His eyes their own brand of muddy blue longing. Five years since, his friend is still a life undeleted, peering from under horn-rimmed glasses. Four walls of a coffin or the four walls of a display picture? Find me the difference. A man shifts in a quasi-dream called afterlife.</p>
<p>My father's cufflinks, cold and dulled, on a drawer desk a dead man bought him for a wedding gift. The heat of a pavement turns xalwo into caramel into plasma. </p>
<p>The old poets said home was a woman. Only a woman can bleed this much without dying. Maybe home is a man's lust ticking under a vest, leaving us to pick up the pieces.</p>

<p>Imagine a rage that needs to spread like that? </p>

The unthought has a comb

Friday night communion looks like washing your hair as the
　　water swallows your people.
Do it anyway. Two picks at hand, *MANUFACTURED IN
　　NIGERIA,*
the teeth a fine row of discipline. Remind me. It hurts. It
　　should.
Olive oil to drip down the elbows, the good stuff,
poured how you were taught. Slicken down the pauses.
　　Shea-spit mix
for the baby hairs,
set the helical right down to the lid.
Mama gave you a head of hair to write about.
The kind that's a second passport. We all nurse our
　　blessings.
You turn on the news stream. Watch a newborn dangle
　　between his mother's legs,
sinking like a stone. The sea his first taste of salt.
This too, a blessing. A woman splits herself apart, an ankle
　　in each time zone.
A meaning in none.

There is no 'us'. You, untangling, from inside an island,
the child of rolled dice and fluke,
collapsing yourself into a guilt,
made for your own longing.

Claim nothing more than each knuckle's crack, the Lord's
　　work in each braid,
pulled to the quick. Loop a finger in coil and split
the shore in half. Bring back those who left.

All their small deaths line the dressing table,
balanced on its lip, and floating.
Prick the greased scalp awake. Takes a good hour, sometimes
more,
to set the waves in motion.

Asmara Road, NW2

I have no name for what is throbbing in our cheeks.

This place numbed our fathers
with its rehearsals of grieving. It won't take us too.
They don't tell you how criminally boring exile is.
I mean, I hate to be underwhelmed,
but this evening's dying sun won't allow that.
Neither will the molten light,
the heat a ripe fist against our napes.

'I feel like R&B & milk' Amirah says, crossing then uncrossing
her legs by the bus stop, facing the cemetery. We laugh as old
     bones dry.
In a field opposite, Rugby Club boys nuzzle against each other's
     necks,
their giggles like swinging gates.

Here is where an afternoon eats its meal from the hollow
of elbow pits.

Here is all the uneventful, all the safe, our parents came here for.

Here is the dark spiral of our beginnings.

DEGNA STONE

■ **DEGNA STONE** is a poet and producer based in Gateshead, originally from the Midlands. She is co-founder and Managing Editor of *Butcher's Dog* poetry magazine and is an Assistant Editor at *The Rialto*. She received a Northern Writers' Award in 2015 and holds an MA in Creative Writing from Newcastle University. ■

▪ LIZ BERRY:

One of the most beguiling things about Degna's poems is their constant pull towards the dark seam of life. These are poems that seek to conjure mysteries and to push into the troubling and unsettling cracks in society. An engaging and compelling performer with a strong concern for social and political justice, Degna has taken the urgency and directness of her theatre and spoken-word background and brought them to the page with a bold spareness and power.

Now resident in the North East, Degna describes herself as a 'Midlander in self-imposed exile', and this desire to simultaneously explore and push away from the place where she grew up informs much of her work. She is drawn to the underbelly of urban life and this troubling element often creeps into her poems through the suggestion of folklore or myth: the secret graveyard beyond the carefully built housing estate, the sinister botanical flora which stifles a beloved's mechanical heart. Her poems are fascinated by the experiences of women – young girls, wives and mothers – and the dangers they navigate and rise against. Her new extended prose poem sequence, *A Lick of Me Shoe*, extracted here, is her most exciting and ambitious project yet: a narrative of a chaotic working class girlhood in the West Midlands is interwoven with Tamworth's Saxon history and the story of its warrior queen, Æthelflæd, Lady of the Mercians.

As an editor, Degna has spoken of her passion for discovering 'poems that are a call to action…poems that make what is happening in the world more bearable'. This same commitment drives her practice, urging her to strive to create poems that challenge and unsettle the reader, raising questions about social injustice and complacency. Her poems are restrained and unsettling, pulling back from sentiment even when writing of family and relationships. As befits an editor, her eye for the clean and tough line are superb. She has written previously of her desire in writing to 'go beyond what is possible now' and the poems here show us a poet already on that thrilling journey. ■

Swimming

Knowing that we
were not what we wanted,
       we strayed

miles from anyone
who would care
       if we went in too far.

We pulled each other further in,
neck deep, the river bed
       slipshifting under our feet.

The water stripped our skin,
nerve ends shut down

       we were raw.

I waited for you to resurface,
looked back at the space
       where you should have been –

when they pulled
us out

       we were dazed.

from A Lick of Me Shoe

She is told to keep quiet so she'll spend her days mute. She will stay away from school and her friends. She will stay silent. She will watch from her hiding place behind Æthelflæd's statue. She will learn how to evade, drop off the radar. She will resurface in the system fifteen years later. And they'll wonder why they never saw her coming.

*

She unlatches her bedroom window and climbs out onto the porch roof, down to street level and walks the three miles into town. She's tall, for her age, so she doesn't look out of place walking though the council estate alone. Feral kids with fox faces blend into the brickwork. Nothing, no one to see here. The walls she's left behind are smeared with shit. A dirty protest at being locked in, rough messages drawn in waste.

*

The sun pushes her towards the dark waters of the Tame. She doesn't need to be told, she knows if she walks along the river bed she can hold her breath as long as she needs. She reaches the place where the Swans hold court. They dip their heads under the water and speak to her without saying a word. She asks them if she can stay and they don't say no. They tell her they can break a man's neck, if he gets too close.

*

91

Æthelflæd knows how to hold a sword. Knows how to cleave a man almost in two. She loves the smell of blood in battle and it fills her dreams. She is glad she doesn't live in peaceful times.

*

The Peelers have been informed. They find her. Bring her home to her room (all traces of its lock removed), to the messages on the wall (that have been Dettolled clean). When they leave he takes a fan belt from his tool box. Beats her. Welts bursting over her skin.

*

She keeps space between them. Wills it to take physical form, fills it with a wide river. Icy. Deep. Rip currents will drag him under if he tries to cross. Her breath gathers in the top part of her chest like it's ready to roar, ready to blast him if he tries to get close. Outside the street lights have bleached the colour from everything.

*

She is building a mountain that will rise between her bed and the bedroom door. It is slow, secret work. It will be unscaleable. It will be made up of snot rags, used tampons, week-old pizza crust found under the wardrobe, the mould that forms on the surface of tea dregs. The things that no one wants to touch. She'll reinforce it with torn homework, dirty pissy sheets, cheap toys that broke on the first playing. There will be a hidden tunnel for her sister.

*

We are hard to tolerate. Our behaviour inexplicable. We keep ourselves closed, never smile. We are attention seekers. Not 'Look at me! Look at me!' but 'Look at how we are living. Will you help us?' We are hard to control. Easy to manipulate. We are thieves, truants, scrappers, vandals. Trying to get what we don't, what we can't, have. We gather in packs, smoke fags, spit on floors. We are loud. We are waiting to be found.

Mr Stone's Bionic Heart

Subacute Bacterial Endocarditis (SBE) is a bacterial infection
that produces growths on the endocardium (the cells lining
the inside of the heart)... and, if untreated, can become fatal
within six weeks to a year.

The sound of your heart beating
could be heard across a room.

I thought it beat so loudly for me
but you explained: a mechanical valve

had replaced the dilating aorta
that would have killed you

if you had lived without diagnosis,
that I could hear a surgical steel

ball bearing thunking into place on each beat
to stop blood regurgitating into your heart.

That first night I took a valium so I could sleep
with my head on your chest.

Years later, the night before you collapsed,
I didn't notice how quiet your heartbeat was.

Two days into your hospital stay
we couldn't hear it at all –

the surgeon talked through your chances,
described the process of weeding

the vegetation growing inside its chambers.
Your bionic heart had let us down.

The River Gods

We don't believe in river gods.
Don't fight for the souls

washed out with the floods.
We don't pray.

We gather in packs, congregate in bars
where liquor is cheaper than water.

We drink. We fight.
We fuck in alleyways,

fake orgasms for a city
that doesn't know who we are.

We are chased to the river's edge,
sacrifice the contents of our stomachs

to icons built in steel, forms
that span the water like pagan priests.

We try to reconcile ourselves
with reflections distorted in thick currents –

What will happen if
we let the water take us home?

We're not afraid of river gods.
Don't fight for the souls

washed out with the floods.
We don't believe.

Cross Bones Burial Ground

[Since then, each night contains all others]

Dried up roses faded to brown,
a handmade, Red Cross flag
tied between the square bars of the gate,

champagne corks, raffia bows,
whatever these Southwark mourners
had to hand to show they care.

It looks like the site of a stabbing
or an industrial accident,
another post-Diana shrine.

Coming back that way late one night,
caught up in a procession for *the outcast dead*
I learned its meaning.

I threaded the smooth silver key-ring you gave me
onto a piece of greyed-out red ribbon,
left your memory there.

YOMI SODE

■ **YOMI SODE** balances the fine line between Nigerian and British cultures, sometimes humorous, loving, self-reflective and uncomfortable. Over the past nine years, he has had work commissioned by The Mayor's Office, BBC World Service/Africa, Channel4, the UN Humanitarian Summit and various other charities. In 2014, he won a place on Nimble Fish's RE: Play programme to begin developing his one-man show *COAT*. The scratch was programmed in festivals held by Southbank Centre and Roundhouse, to sold-out audiences, and the complete show debuted in 2017.

In 2016 Yomi travelled to New York City as part of the British Council's Shakespeare Lives initiative to read his work at the New York Public Library. Outside of his creative endeavours, Yomi has spent the past 16 years working with at-risk young people and their families, teaching in schools, providing crisis mediation, and facilitating workshops on gangs, sexual health and drugs awareness.

He is the founder of The Daddy Diaries, a website dedicated to giving Fathers/Guardians the opportunity to share their stories and build a support system with other Fathers/Guardians. ■

■ W.N. HERBERT:

Yomi Sode's work manages to bring quite different – indeed contrary – subjects and poetic energies into a marvellous equilibrium. On the one hand there is the rich subject matter of his Nigerian heritage, balancing mythopoetic gods from the Orisha pantheon with a complex sociopolitical reality; on the other there are the difficult gulfs of race and gender politics in contemporary Britain which also must, somehow, be negotiated. Each clashes with each with, often, violent consequences:

> Witnesses recall you bloodied and exhausted,
>
> looking at your swollen knuckles saying
> *what did I do?* repetitively
>
> as if you were a toy wound for entertaining.

He accomplishes this dextrous balancing act over that dangerous drop with the requisite apparent ease. Mastery of structure, that crucial skill, is demonstrated through the variety of his verse forms, from the countdown of lines in 'After life' to its final gnomic monostich, to the irony of 'The Exhibition', with its icy curatorial engagements with race. Throughout, proverbial phrases from Yoruba play against the stark, even shocking, contexts of his poetry.

This is writing which performs brilliantly, but you are never allowed to forget that much more is at stake: our inner integrities and outer identities are exposed as seeking an easy reconciliation which poem after poem refuses to grant them. All is kept, nimbly, in the air, and nothing may be relied on – except, as in the triumphant mesh of prose poem, grime lyric and Yoruba phrase that is 'Distant Daily *Ijó*', the dancer's trust in the dance.

In that trust, however, he sees the seeds of a deeper engagement with, and an expanded awareness of, our better natures.

The Exhibition

We'll let you take the evidence into consideration for yourself
below

JAY ELECTRONICA

Exhibit A

She places her finger on my chin and starts her motion down-
wards. In her excitement, she says she's *never been with a
Black man*; as if tonight she is committing a grave sin. Asking
about my size and whether it's true, whether / *once you go
Black, you never go back.*

> I will be her best secret,
> covered in oil.
> Hanging / like her jaw.

Exhibit B

You waited / until our colleagues left the office and shared
the hatred you've had for Black people for so long. So much
so you paid an additional £300 a month to ensure your child-
ren would not encounter one.

> Father / the people of Charleston prayed
> for Dylann Roof this morning.
>
> They sung loud for the camera as though
> your love was vengeful enough.
>
> Each tear fell like bodies
> of their loved ones that evening.

Exhibit C

The kettle boils while you share your latest analogy with us.
Your daughter / raised on feminist principles set by yourself;
discloses a conversation (heard on a bus) between a group of
boys over the weekend. *She told me and my husband, we*
couldn't believe it. The appalling way they spoke about women,
the rap language they used. Disgusting!

The kettle / still boiling, mimicked my response.
That precise second you ended, without a word
I watched you / swim into each sentence,
rearranging the letters, the meaning.
Without a word, just a stare.

Wọn Ti Dé

Oyá, our dead gradually make their way,
bodies still warm from the gutting.

As you arrive, give her your names,
Damilola, Carl, Mohammad, Derek.

Oyá, remind them of a home that resides
in the *èkó* sand between their toes,

show each of your stillborn
wrapped around your waist,

èyin ọmọ ololorun, when walking to your graves,
hold her hand in calming your pierced hearts.

Oyá, are they scared as your gates open?
I would suggest you train some to be warriors,

though I doubt they knew
what they fought for whilst on earth.

Oyá,
Yansán

Ọyá – Iyansan
guard them, as you would your own.

The Outing

Onlookers witnessed your wrath that night
how your fist rose to the heavens,

striking down as if Ṣango lived within you.
Thirty going on thirty-one. I wasn't sure what to say.

I've never been here.
The papers described him as tall.

They said his neck broke before he landed
as if his body was a Slinky, waiting

for the rest of him to hit the ground.
Witnesses recall you bloodied and exhausted,

looking at your swollen knuckles saying
what did I do? repetitively

as if you were a toy wound for entertaining.
Uncle Elijah believes mental health is a *western thing*.

He says back home, elders would out those who were cursed
and banish them from the village. I sit with you, old friend.

We break silence with passive laughs as if we were sat
with our fathers. Then silence again.

Night Terrors

Do you see how many invitations I decline,
butting shirt hangers onto each other?

Each 'how are you finding it?' reminds me
night terrors carry little weight.

In this darkness, the street lamp writes
on our sparse wall like an epiphany.

I rock our boy to sleep, feel my stomach fold
over my belt. The excess fat slowly engulfs

the buckle like my father's. Tonight,
like most nights, growing old scares me.

The Man Behind the Switch

Lẹ́hin òkunkun biribiri imọ́lẹ̀ á tan – After darkness there is light.

Aunty's neighbour cried while tipping her pot of Egusi stew[1] into
the waste.
Tonight, her children's stomachs ache a little longer as the sun settles
on Delmont Holmes. Fathers return from work, children look for
sandals,
calling across balconies, imitating the heightened conversations
heard through windowpanes, Mothers knot the curtains.
We hear the crows before seeing them, their unruly cackle
into moonlit hours that scare toddlers back home, crackles
heard over televisions, radios, political debates

then it happens. Little is known about this man behind the switch.
The elders follow Aunty's torch like moths to Iṣọ́ òru[2]
children sing in the silence, wishing for electricity like rain.
Nepa[3] e mú iná wá, e mú iná wá o.[4] This man behind the switch,
whether small or fat, whether he has a heart, *ẹ má binu.*[5]
Seventeen hours pass in this lantern filled darkness, we still wait.

1. Nigerian delicacy made from spinach and ground seeds
2. Night Vigil
3. National Electric Power Authority
4. Nepa bring the light back, bring the light back
5. Don't be angry

Distant Daily *Ijó*

(A response to 'Mingus Music Act 1' by Ronnie McGrath)

With my music / I create change / I am using my music as a weapon
FELA KUTI

The nesting of *igbó* smoke in tangled unruly kinks /

the testosterone wiped off foreheads / listening to these sounds
bí confessions guiding us through the night / our pupils tuck
into themselves upon confrontation / or aligns *àwọ̀n ārā wā*
for survival /

> *Think you're a big boy cos you go gym* [1] /

knuckles grind more than teeth / bass strums the thinnest of
veins / I wonder why this body contorts to each melodic drop /
turning the insides of my stomach how spatulas do pancakes /
why I head nod in *ijó* as if each gun finger shot above pierces
clouds before reaching a half lit moon / a libation of bodies /
why I'm arms out in *ijó* / palm striking walls damp from a
defeated week in ritual / stinging hands that sing / singeing
ash on each other's skin / too drunk to give two fucks / my
àdúrà / a something on Sundays / in exchange for lyrics that
feel closer to the ends / I have yet to see a parting of seas
but I've witnessed riots and still fear police / that fear this
body / *ọwọ́ wā* / dry and unloved / yet they stretch like vines
to Gods that look and dress like us /

> *Murder charge aint a joke and laugh / you think that you're
> shower, but you can't even jump in the bath* [2] /

mò ngbọ èyí with deceased friends / then wake to relish timed
moments with the living / so when you chant grime / but

have never cut a toothpaste in half and struggled to squeeze
out its remains / you are merely a fan / I will out dance that
fetish / I will skank / outline its splatter of appropriation in
chalk / I will dance / flexing this arm / bending this knee /
in this derelict space / love is a musky current in the room
you dare not question / as though they don't exist /

*Even if I had a big house in the country / I wouldn't stay
caged up like a monkey* [3] /

master of ceremonies / you carry the heart of a trumpeter /
the beat is not just a beat / it is this *èmí* / jumping from
body to body / the soundtrack of an offering / *wá* and feel
this / skin rippling music / galvanised chaos / heat drenching
clothes as though summer never left music / each note is a
reminder / a name / a knife wound / a scream / a revol-
ution / never music to dance your cares away to / this vio-
lence your children listen to / young Mark Duggan's *boy
dem* stop and search to / such Mingus in this music / scaling
our bones like piano keys / doing a distant daily *ijó* of head
nods / nine to five and overtime / *ijó* of bass and more bass /
ijó of praise to the DJ / *ijó* of the rage we share the moment
a track gets a wheel up /

ijó of the barrel load / the cocking back of steel / the *pop,
pop pop* [4]! /   A pause / the stampede of people /
a search for those close / a quick feel of this *árá* / a deeper
breath / the exalted feeling it wasn't you / and we're out [5] /

ask me why I find home in a place I could die /

I will rep grime until I'm in my grave
GHETTS

108

GLOSSARY

igbó – cannabis / weed
bí – like
àwọ̄n ārā wā – our bodies
ijó – dance
àdúrà – prayer
ọwọ́ wā – our hands
mò ngbọ èyí – I hear this
wá – come
ẹ̀mí – spirit
ārā – body
boy dem – police
wheel up – a rewind from a DJ

1. D Double E, Emcee
2. Skepta, Emcee
3. Wiley, Emcee
4. Kano, Emcee
5. Kano, Emcee

After life

ìbínú ò mọ̀ pé olúwa òun ò lẹ́sẹ̀ nlẹ̀
Anger does not know that its owner has no legs to stand on.

6. Four men brought a cow to its knees.
    Slicing its throat amidst the struggle.
    Then placing a bucket for blood to
    pour into. I am sure God heard that cry.
    That plea for life. Still, tonight,
    our families will feast.

5. The bottle thrown in the sky has no wings,
    just a bird's eye view of violence.
    A rejection from unloving hands,
    spinning in unknotted air
    to a death it never saw coming.

4. It's easier to shoot a man than to stab him.
    You stab him? go in deep and twist.
    You twist to leave it open then pull out,
    it will be messy.

3. Another murder on the news as we stuff our faces full.
    Mum believes that church redeems sinners, though
    they have robbed, harmed or killed.

2. *Why is Derek always like this?*
    I don't know. It must be in his food or something.

1. Some believe death resurrects in many forms.

JENNIFER LEE TSAI

■ **JENNIFER LEE TSAI** is a British poet of Chinese heritage. She was born in Bebington on the Wirral peninsula and grew up in Liverpool. She studied English Language and Literature at St Andrews, and later, for an MA in English Literature from Liverpool University. She completed an MA in Creative Writing (Poetry) with Distinction from the University of Manchester's Centre for New Writing in 2015. She has worked extensively as an English language tutor in both further and higher education. Her poems have been published in *Smoke*, *The Rialto* and elsewhere. ■

■ KAREN McCARTHY WOOLF:

Jennifer Lee Tsai's poems have an ethereal, ghostly quality that wafts onto the page, through Gothic churchyards and Liverpool's immortalised Penny Lane to the temples and *dim sum* cafés of Hong Kong, rising like steam from a bamboo basket. That is not to say that their subjects are insubstantial: the difficulties of love, longing, loss and belonging are all thrown up into the air and allowed to take flight.

There is also an element of travelogue at play, as evidenced in the prose poem 'New Territories', which captures the paradoxes of the second-generation search for identity, when 'the past and present collide' ('A Certain Purity of Light') often to unexpected or inconclusive effect. This poem is also something of an *ars poetica*: 'I want to understand something about the nature of emptiness, return to the idea of nothing-ness, start again somehow' it declares. In this sense Tsai is a philosopher and a diviner – sometimes of white space in the sky, sometimes of white space on the page, sometimes of red walls in an attic room. She is a poet who seeks to decipher symbols, whether from Jane Eyre, the I-Ching, a 70s disco glitter ball or a 'Chinese pictogram of a cloud at sunset' ('Parkgate') and reinterpret them within her own realm of familial, platonic and sexual relationships, with the quest for self-discovery and perhaps, personal transformation or even redemption, at the core.

The word 'perhaps' is a key to Tsai's poetics: she is not a writer willing to settle on false certainties, opting instead to delve into the uncharted possibilities of coincidence, synchron-icity and even birdsong as a transcendent force with the capacity to connect us to our ancestors in a manner that more conventional, physical means cannot. In part, Tsai's literary strategy is to afford equal status to both the spiritual and physical planes, so that history, myth and contemporary narrative might coalesce across continents and eras. There is also a dreamlike quality to her work, whether the narrator is describing a literal dream or another, remembered scenario, where the relationships of light and shadow are metaphors for an emotional palette that flickers between hope, despair, rage and acceptance. It is in this regard that I find Tsai's work remarkable: for its honesty and insistence in pursuing both intimate and universal truths, however uncomfortable or elusive they may be. But it is the slipperiness of life that preoccupies and how we might, albeit briefly, hold it in our gaze for a moment of sublime or agonising contemplation. Perhaps we are immersed in the autobiography of the writer, perhaps we are witnessing a partially fictitious refigurement of a (dis)embodied self. Perhaps. The answer being less important than the question, the reveal a mysterious and therefore compelling blur between apparition and event. Tsai is a writer who treads an uncompromising and precarious balance between visibility and absence, and it is this scope of her ambition that makes her brave. As she states in 'Doppelgänger':

> Twilight she comes alive,
> pirouettes like fire.
> In the morning, she leaves;
> she can come and go, as she pleases.

New Territories

When I first got off the plane, the heat hit me, tropical, alien. Everyone here is Chinese, I'm no different, for once. The anonymity subdues me. This is where my past begins. At 7am, I meet my uncle for steamed bamboo baskets of *dim sum* and oolong tea. He is tall, fair-skinned, his features more Eurasian, almost like a *gweilo*, people say. From my aunt's apartment windows, tendrils of mist rise from Tai Mo Shan mountain, mammoth dragonflies hover, translucent-winged, their presence signalling the imminent fall of rain. I look for traces of my grandmother. A woman I meet, from the same village as her, mourns for the three children she left behind, laments the tyrant husband, the cruelty of the mother-in-law. She remembers my mother as a child. By day, I read the *Tao Te Ching*. I want to understand something about the nature of emptiness, return to the idea of nothingness, start again somehow. The character for Tao contains a head and a walking foot which means the way, the path or the road. In the Chi Lin nunnery on Diamond Hill, there are lotus ponds, bonsai tea plants, purple and orange bougainvillea. Behind intricate screens of mystery, nuns offer fruit and rice to Buddha, or chant. High-rise apartments tower in the background.

Parkgate

We share part of the same first name, my cousin and I:
a Chinese pictogram of a cloud at sunset,
burning bright orange or violet-gold;
within it, the character for rain.
How close we were, living almost as sisters...

so much so, I told strangers that we were,
wanting someone to protect me,
if only in an imagined reality.
Then, we lived in an old restaurant,
Tudor-like with its half-timbered façade.

I was six, she was eight. My father, the manager –
gone awol, mother weeping in the bathroom.
Empty afternoons, colouring pictures
on the dining tables, watching koi and angelfish
in an aquarium placed for feng-shui.

We'd traipse along the promenade with its ice
cream shops, fresh shrimps and cockles. Today
at the same restaurant in a darkened
interior, with cups of jasmine tea, we stare
at the marsh – a hinterland on the coastline

of the Dee estuary. The sky opening up.
Once, this used to be a port, an exit point
for Ireland. During high tide, water reaches
the sandstone sea wall; hen-harriers dive
as merlins pursue. Beyond, the Welsh hills.

Spring brings skylarks weaving their nests,
golden samphire and scurvy-grass.
When we leave, I see that same flight of stairs
leading to another room; we shouldn't have entered
all that time ago. We flew up and down those stairs,

trying to catch each other, stop from falling. Upstairs,
there was a bar, a disco, a silver glitter-ball.
We dressed up in my mother's clothes and stilettos,
smearing lipstick on rose-bud mouths;
the line shifting around what we knew and didn't know.

They say that geishas inhabit another realm –
a flower and willow world. It's so cold.
Did I lure you in? Was it my fault we got lost?
I shouldn't have been leading the way,
never was very good with directions.

The Valley Spirit Never Dies

The Valley Spirit never dies,
and is called Mysterious Female.

LAO TZU, *Tao Te Ching*

My aunt speaks in the dialect
of the Hakka tribe,
a language I do not fully understand;
Chinese gypsies, like dandelions,
they flourish in adverse soil,
refuse to be trampled on,
the women's feet un-bound.

She rises early in the morning,
a hollow bamboo reed
filled with infinite energy;
dresses in dark, loose trousers, oriental blouse,
a black-veiled hat.
She remembers, she remembers,
lights incense, replenishes the bowls of oranges,

white chrysanthemums on the ancestral altar;
praying for our memories of the dead.
At night, she tries to tell me what she saw –
1961, living in the same village
as my grandmother, in New Territories,
who, one day, drank weed killer
by the harbour at Sha Tau Gok.

Later that day, we visit a temple
to honour the gods of literature and of war;
two banyan wishing trees in the courtyard,
their branches strewn with coloured streamers,
fluttering desires. My fires are renewed
and I feel her in my bones,
I hear her in the songs of birds.

Black Star

He was everything I hadn't wished for.
He opened up, like foxgloves do, and sucked me in.
He was a name I couldn't say,
a train journey I shouldn't have gone on.

He was a crow crowing over me,
His smile was bulletproof, flashing six gold teeth.
His energy sang in the empty spaces he left,
like the chimes of Buddhist bells.

A Certain Purity of Light

I

Where was I?

And what was I?

Standing in the umbra of your shadow, your conjurings.
Forgetting my own magic.
I descended so deep

into darkness, black on black.

A cloud of not-knowing, wandering in a fugue. The sacristy
of my mind
overcame me, and yes, I admit – I was truly lost.
The nigredo of your corvine heart fucked me up for years –
ten, to be exact.
I should have heeded those spindrift voices.

II

My grandmother that I never knew,
how I miss you.
how and what were you?
I invoke your spirit,
make offerings
to the Three Mountain Kings

III

The white morning
curdles its fury
as only October can.

I assemble fragments in disarray.

The light coruscates in the Georgian quarter.
I'm on Hope Street.
Before me, the Anglican cathedral looms; Gothic in its
    sandstone façade.
Seagulls flitter by.

IV

On Huskisson Street, they say there's a ghost – a man with no
    face.
Some nights, you can hear the ringing of sword blades
    duelling.

Once, in your attic, I saw pieces of the women you had loved
and who had loved you.

I had no designs on you.

Half-crazy, because I've been made to feel so.

V

I had abandoned myself utterly;
I was a paper doll.
If you had held me up to the light,
it would have shone through.

Now all I can do is laugh.

The dragon in me has returned.

VI

There is a certain purity of light
that arises
on these almost-winter days,
violet but not quite.
Times, when the past and the present collide.

VII

The day slides into view.
My love arrives.
On Catharine Street,
we drink a beer or two.

VIII

Sometimes, there are nightmares still.
I wake up suddenly from a feeling
that I'm *there* again.
Trapped in that red attic room.

IX

The curtain sways in the night.
I reach over,
feel the warmth of your nakedness,
your body next to mine.

Going Home

I

On this cobalt night, the 15th day of the 8th month,
the moon is a perfect circle, bone-white.
Look closely, you might see that dark speck
on the surface is the moon-goddess, *Chang'e*.

In ancient times, there were ten suns
scorching the earth.
The archer, *Houyi*, shot down nine of them,
received two elixirs of immortality.

One day, his wife found them, swallowed both,
floated upwards into the sky,
her robes flowing behind her.
She became air and light and sound.

II

On such a night, Li Po dreamt of his home.
The harvest moonlight glimmered in his room
like frost on the ground,
trying to capture the moon's reflection in a lake, he died,

one of the Eight Immortals of the Wine Cup,
just as you, my father, always longed for your home
on late nights fuelled by whisky, *hieng-ha* – your village.
I wondered where this was, what China was like,

listening to stories you told me – in Guangdong,
you used to skip school, escaping, to catch fish in the stream.
I remember the painting you had: a Chinese junk
across a sunset harbour, the picture from Hong Kong

you gave me: two pandas – a parent clasping its child
on a celadon background, bamboo,
mountains in the distance,
to the side: black ink calligraphy.

III

Father, on the 15th day of the 8th month, I returned.
And where is the heart?
I wonder, as I re-trace my steps
in time to a grey Liverpool,

nothing out of the ordinary;
arriving home on an 80A bus
down Rose Lane that Saturday afternoon
to find you slumped in your leather armchair –

a yellow fleece caught over your head like a net.
You said you'd be travelling the world,
perhaps among the sapphire rivers, pagodas
jade mountains and lotus flowers of your youth…

I have been away so long, and you will be leaving soon.

Doppelgänger

I've tried endless entreaties,
offered green tea sweetened with rose and lily,
even dainty cups of osmanthus wine
but none of this appeases; she shrugs her shoulders,
a real crazy-maker, slides down the banisters,
half-drunk mugs of mocha on window sills, light-switches on,
taps running, door unlocked, her Arabian perfume oil of
     amber and oud –
origami-ing out of books and magazines.
Twilight, she comes alive,
pirouettes like fire.
In the morning, she leaves;
she can come and go, as she pleases.

RAYMOND ANTROBUS

■ **RAYMOND ANTROBUS** is a British-Jamaican poet, performer and educator, born and bred in East London, Hackney. He is one of the world's first recipients of an MA in Spoken Word education from Goldsmith's University.

His poems have been published/forthcoming in *Poetry*, *Wasafiri*, *The Rialto*, *Magma* and The Deaf Poets Society. His first pamphlet, *Shapes & Disfigurements of Raymond Antrobus* (2012), is published by Burning Eye Books. His second, *To Sweeten Bitter* (2017), is published by Outspoken Press. His debut poetry collection will be published by Penned in the Margins (2018).

Raymond is co-curator of popular London poetry events Chill Pill (Soho Theatre and The Albany) and Keats House Poets Forum. Raymond's poetry has appeared on BBC 2 and BBC Radio 4, in the *Big Issue*, *Jamaica Gleaner* and *Guardian*, and at TedxEastEnd.

Sky Arts and Ideas Tap listed Raymond in the top 20 promising young artists in the UK. ■

■ HANNAH LOWE:

Raymond Antrobus' poetry is charged by inbetweenness. It thrives on the space between worlds. In some poems, these worlds are the before and after of his father's death. In others, it's the space between hearing and deafness; or the space between Hackney where Ray grew up, and Jamaica, his father's home; or the space between the now of now and the then-ness of childhood. The inbetweeness of mixed race is another liminal space in Ray's poetic concerns – to have a black father and white mother but look perhaps like both, perhaps neither. From these spaces – call them tensions or catalysts – arises a questioning, journeying, political and personal poetry.

In turns tender, in turns angry, Ray's poems resound with specificity – brands names, rap lyrics, colours, smells, the names of soul tunes, the sound of his father crooning. But sound itself is also a contested thing in Ray's work, often made strange, as in his beautiful synesthetic description of the 'noiseless palace' of deafness 'where the doorbell is puls-ating / light and I am able to answer' ('Echo'). Ray is also an experimenter and inventor, pushing his writing into new shapes, playing with forms, working the white space of the page. Yet at the heart of the writing there is simplicity, pre-cision and clean metaphor, like the word of his father which 'is not dead', but carried 'like sugar / on a silver spoon / up the Mobay Hills/past the flaked white walls/of plantation houses ('To Sweeten Bitter').

Crucial to Ray's work is his experience and training as a spoken word educator, as one of the first graduates as Gold-smith's innovative MA. And Raymond's history with words began across the line, in that wrong-side-of-the-tracks place – the spoken word scene. Ask Ray what he thinks about the divide when you see him. I'm thinking the finished place of a poem should probably always be a spoken one, given out to the world.

In developing his world-view and poetry aesthetics, Ray criss-crosses London to attend readings, lectures, debates. He's a listening poet, and he always has a new book in his hand. In fact, Ray is my go-to man for new poetry recommendations, like the US Break Beat poets he introduced to me. Ask Ray what the poets in Ghana are doing these days, and he might well know.

Enjoy these readable, speakable poems. ■

To Sweeten Bitter

My father had four children
and three sugars in his coffee
and every birthday he bought me
a dictionary which got thicker
and thicker and because his word
is not dead, I carry it like sugar

on a silver spoon
up the Mobay hills in Jamaica
past the flaked white walls
of plantation houses
past canefields and coconut trees
past the new crystal sugar factories.

I ask dictionary why we came here
it said nourish so I sat with my aunt
on her balcony at the top
of Barnet Heights
and ate salt fish
and sweet potato

and watched women
leading their children
home from school
as I ate I asked dictionary
what is difficult about love?
It opened on the word *grasp*

and I looked at my hand
holding this ivory knife

and thought about how hard it was
to accept my father
for who he was
and where he came from

how easy it is now to spill
sugar on the table before
it is poured into my cup.

Echo

1

My ear amps whistle like they are singing
to Echo, goddess of noise,
the ravelled knot of tongues,
of blaring birds, consonant crumbs
of dull door bells, sounds swamped
in my misty hearing aid tubes.
Gaudí believed in holy sound
and built a cathedral to contain it,
pulling hearing men from their knees
as though atheism is a kind of deafness.
Who would turn down God?
Even though I have not heard
the golden decibel of angels,
I have been living in a noiseless
palace where the doorbell is pulsating
light and I am able to answer.

2

What?

a word that keeps looking
in mirrors like it is in love
with its own volume.

What?

I am a one-word question,
a one-man
patience test.

What?

What language
would we speak
without ears?

What?

Is paradise
a world where
I hear everything?

What?

How will my brain
know what to hold
if it has too many arms?

3

The day I cleared out my dead father's flat,
I throw boxes of moulding LPs, Garvey,
Malcolm X, Mandela, speeches on vinyl.
I find a TDK cassette tape on the shelf,
smudged green label *Raymond Speaking*.

I play the tape in his vintage cassette player
and hear my two-year-old voice chanting my name *Antrob*
and dad's laughter crackling in the background
not knowing I couldn't hear the word 'bus'
and I wouldn't until I got my hearing aids.
Now I sit here listening to the space of deafness –
Antrob Antrob Antrob

4

And no one knew what I was missing
until a doctor gave me a handful of Lego
and said to put a brick on the table
every time I heard a sound.
After the test I still held enough bricks
in my hand to build a house
and call it my sanctuary,
call it the reason I sat in saintly silence
during my grandfather's sermons when he preached
The Good News, I only heard
as Babylon's babbling echoes.

5

> And if you don't catch nothing
> then something wrong with your ears –
> they been tuned to de wrong frequency.
>
> KEI MILLER

So maybe I belong to the universe
underwater, where all songs
are smeared wailings for Salacia,
goddess of saltwater, healer
of infected ears, which is what the doctor
thought I had since deafness
did not run in the family
but came from nowhere,
so they syringed in olive oil
and saltwater, and we all waited
to see what would come out.

Jamaican British

(after Arron Samuels)

Some people would deny that I'm Jamaican British.
Angelo nose. Hair straight. No way I can be Jamaican British.

They think I say I'm black when I say Jamaican British
but the English boys at school made me choose Jamaican, British?

Half-caste, half mule, house slave – Jamaican British.
Light skin, straight male, privileged – Jamaican British.

Eat callaloo, plantain, jerk chicken – I'm Jamaican
British don't know how to serve our dishes, they enslaved us.

In school I fought a boy in the lunch hall – Jamaican.
At home, told Dad *I hate dem, all dem Jamaicans* – I'm British.

He laughed, said you cannot love sugar and hate your sweetness,
took me straight to Jamaica – passport, British.

Cousins in Kingston called me Jah-English,
proud to have someone in their family – British.

Plantation lineage, world war service, how do I serve Jamaican
    British?
When knowing how to war is Jamaican
                                        British

LEONARDO BOIX

■ **LEONARDO BOIX** was born in Buenos Aires, Argentina in 1975, and since 1997 has lived in London and Deal, Kent. He read Latin American Studies at Birkbeck College, University of London, where he also gained an MA in Latin American Literature and Culture. He studied at The Poetry School in London with Tamar Yoseloff, Roddy Lumsden and Clare Pollard. As a journalist, Boix has regularly published in the *Guardian*, *Morning Star* and *Miami Herald*, as well as being the correspondent for major Latin American journals and newspapers including *Revista Proceso* (Mexico), *Diario Perfil* (Argentina), and *El Telégrafo* (Ecuador).

Boix is a founding member of SLAP (Spanish and Latin American Poets and Writers in the UK), and as part of this group he has read publicly on many occasions, including at the Poetry Café, Royal Academy of Dramatic Arts (RADA), Unison, Rich Mix and the Deal Poetry Festival (Poesía en la Playa), with readings in Spanish and English.

In 2015 Boix published his first Spanish collection *Un lugar propio* (Letras del Sur, Bs. As.), followed in 2016 by *Mar de noche* (Letras del Sur, Bs. As). He also judged and wrote the prologue for the anthology collection *Apología 3* (Poesía porque sí, 2016), showcasing the best young Argentinian poets. In 2016 Boix won first prize in the Anglo-Chilean Society Poetry Competition.

In English his poetry has featured in the pamphlet *All that is Unsaid*, 2015, as well as in the literary journals *minor literature [s]*, *Azahar Literario*, the *Morning Star* poetry column, *IS&T* and *The Rialto*. Boix is currently working on a collection of poems based on the work of the Dutch painter Hieronymus Bosch, and also on a creative translation of the writings of the Peruvian poet Jorge Eduardo Eialson. ■

■ MICHAEL SCHMIDT:

I have learned a great deal from working with Leonardo Boix on his poems. He is coming into English from Spanish, specifically Argentinean Spanish. In Argentina he has worked as a journalist and published poetry. Like him, I came into English from Spanish (half a century earlier), and some of the challenges he faces are familiar to me.

He is not writing poems about his native Argentina but work rooted in his current experience, and the first substantial poem he shared with me was his 'Ode to Deal' with its unencumbered sense of the English coast. His from-water-to-land points of view (he is a committed swimmer), his evocation of the eccentric, culturally alert house he shares with his artist partner, and the changing weathers of that part of the coast, came across. The editorial challenge was to make the poem more formally itself, to simplify and clarify its movement without losing the freshness of its take on the world. This was done not only by cutting but also by adding back and by working on the metrical patterning to create a firmer correspondence between language and subject, a more effective mimesis.

From the outset Leo was clear about his interest in larger forms, in the poem sequence and the poem series. He can turn unusual lyric poems, but he has a narrative instinct and he is drawn (as I am not) towards ekphrasis. For me this was the most difficult personal, mentorly adjustment. Leo found his bearings in the work of Hieronymus Bosch, one of his actual or adopted ancestors (does it matter?) whose hyper-real surrealism connects with poetic, graphic and spiritual material rooted deep in the poet's imagination. He went to Madrid and spent a long time at the great Bosch exhibition internalising his 'occasions'.

I had no choice but to follow, uttering my fruitless imprecations and my editorial caveats, because this is Leo's adventure and not mine. It is a genuinely exciting quest. I have become increasingly Sancho to his Quixote. I am now fully convinced, as I think he is, too, that the quest is not in vain, and those windmills really are giants. At least some of them are. ■

Pigments alla prima

[a painting technique in which pigments are laid on in one application with little or no underpainting]

Malachite

Hedges of laurel bonariensis, chlorophyll
crawling under our shadows
a little boy poisons ants.

Carmine Lake (Cochineal)

For a giant red flower eating my family
for an exiled animal lost in a walled garden
or a present on your last birthday.

Azurite

A perfect sub-tropical lake
shining blue arms floating
crema del cielo for us kids to devour.

Ivory Black

His empty eyes.
A scared panther in an Argentine circus
whipped by a General holding two cherries.

Lead White

Mother's body resting
a marble emptiness. Was he
also in there trying to escape?

Lead Tin Yellow

Don't assume this, Oriole.
Turn around, in circles
to an ever dying Southern Sun.

Vermilion

Within a hollow Eucalyptus trunk
me, hiding. A language incision
in the shape of a nightmare.

Copper resinate

On this lawn neatly mowed
a verdigris mask. Go back
you are not even English.

Gypsum

Landscape of white
semen, everything that reproduces
won't.

Lime White

A horse crossing an electric ocean
leather bags, some Spanish books
in a desolate departure lounge.

Naples Yellow

My incorrect sun
it lacks smoothness. I burnt once
trying to reach for your forbidden body.

Bone Black

His insides being pulled
the day he crossed the bridge
and never went back.

Carbon Black

Crows grew only
on this side of the map
omens of a new beginning.

Ode to Deal
(Oda a Deal)

I

Morning hour, the humidity of blue hostas,
all leaves for the slugs at dawn.

Foliage, shade-tolerant, perennial,
your nocturnal body wakens next to mine.

In the subtropics I slept defenceless.
Here, the protection of our English bed.

The fear of moths and spiders hiding,
behind our windows, 'castle of saliva'.
Static, the small pond in the sunken garden,
dirty after the pigeons left us.
Pruned hedges of African soapberry,
the waterlily, contained:

I choose each plant with care.
Deciduous, shedding what was no longer needed –

you stare at me, naked, my eyes closed,
magnetic insomnia, sex a slice of charred toast.

II

Oblique sunrise
smoke rising from mines
now closed at Fowlmead.
First hours of day. Again we are up,

barely breathing, the clavichord
plays sweet notes of summer tides,
boiling water for yerba maté –
all in reverse.
I try to speak the language of the country,
the radio replies.
You stare in silence at the flies.

One should learn how to behave!
I touch your hands by mistake.

III

Upstairs, the bedroom: the bedsheets,
a pile of unnecessary clothes, the sea wind
ceaselessly brings in the taste
of salt and leathery seaweed.

We turn the clocks back:
mornings tastes of butter and bad news.
An empty beach
      Mother always longed for in summer,
      she died in the British Hospital,
      opposite Caseros
      the big ombú tree looking on.

IV

Feral seagulls
owls echo down chimneys,
omens of good luck,
they come from the landfills
to die in the sea.

The River Plate always brown,
plains I never saw –
1976. The sea is the sea full of bodies,
in the Southern Hemisphere
the birds sing differently.

I was born at twenty-tree o'clock
in the town of Avellaneda,
other babies cried, jewels stolen
from the General's teeth.

    V

The clouds darken
the mid-morning light,
faded roof tiles, winds
escalate.

A camellia tree trembles.

     In the house where I was born we had
     a tree to hang the washing out
     paving stones always hot,
     dogs barking,
     police on the lookout
                   night and day.

Pablo calls me 'mono-pato': monkey duck.
Your gaze could turn anyone
to dust.

VI

At lunch
the old courtyard wall shadows us,
the jug of water,
plates, salad –
we eat
unconsciously.
I cooked in a dirty pan,
Spanish virgin olive oil,
the chicken slightly off;
pepper-vinegar –
the dressing's yours.

In Argentina since I left the country
the sun went black.
The colours have never returned.

VII

We swim towards the Pier
green blue (Pablo's eyes)
feet touch
the abyss.
A sewage spill
we didn't notice,
the town immobile, limpid, over there:
shed yourself amid
suspended things.

Jellyfish against the rocks.
I tried to bin the gelatine.
Someone shouts:
'In your country I bet you kill animals.'

VIII

Vertical sun,
bathers in ugly colours,
bawling children
and the solid seabird bound
towards the vertiginous blue.
You fall asleep.

> My father lost his only job
> in the factory he had worked at all his life.

> I prefer the salt of my childhood,
> barefoot,
> baked plums burnt sugar.

Our bodies are quite symmetrical.
Did I ever notice this?.

IX

Towards afternoon we un
packed the bag full of sand and stones,
stories of the day,
magazines: tasselled interiors,
suncream for iguanas, scales,
a wet towel hanging from the door,
drying slowly over my sedum succulents.

You're always brown: the porous surface,
salty water when we kiss.
I am in a trance gazing at the bird-feeder
solid as in amber:
both of us contained.

X

The sky explodes in pink,
crisscrossed with swallows,
planes from Heathrow, Luton.
The travellers are finally gone,
we remain
where the light takes us,
bit by bit.

XI

Before dinner you retreat to your studio.
It is full of silver, paintings, drawings
of improbable buildings.
Your ruler for perfect measures,
ink in pots,
you draw while I wait.

We plunge into the darkness
of old Shirley House,
inn for poor mariners.
Nobody's alive. Shipwrecks.
The antique lamps you bought
are lit with care.

We hug for heat.
Let sleep devour us.

I forgot to put the fire out in the fireplace.
        I burnt myself as a child in the old kitchen
        of the summer house in Quequen.
        My grandfather built it with his hands.
        Scars.

XII

After the removal vans have gone
a glacial moon bathes our small library.
We house it in closet rooms.
Books I brought from Argentina,
        memento mori.

The Last Judgement

(Bosch triptych)

Look at my knife   it aches of shininess smoothed   cut it deep
for a present, a last *asado*, your barbecue   in hell or around here
this darkened house   things get lost   not me   bodies pile up
they gave you a year   even   two three four   a second
counted in reverse   a broken egg   he waited for me   down
here last ceremony blackening your eyes *it was a luxury to have you*

Strange roof   she dances naked   snaked twirling   next
to her reptiled   *move the heater closer to*   his legs, his empty eyes
a body that does not recognise   you   I
follow your fluids   your world getting smaller   until
someone calls   she cries   *I'll be alone*   his animals
with musical instruments on their heads   tambourines, a cornet

for a last piece: your skin turned yellow like a leaf, a golden thief, if

■ EDITOR'S BIOGRAPHY:

Karen McCarthy Woolf was born in London to an English mother and Jamaican father, and is a Fellow of The Complete Works I. She is the editor of three literary anthologies, and reviews for numerous journals including *Poetry London*, *The Poetry Review* and *Modern Poetry in Translation*. Her first book, *An Aviary of Small Birds* (Carcanet, 2014) was described as a 'pitch perfect debut' (Kate Kellaway, *Guardian/Observer*) and was a Poetry Book Society Recommendation and short-listed for the Fenton Aldeburgh and Forward first collection prizes.

A recipient of a Glenna Luschei Prize from the American journal *Prairie Schooner*, Karen has read her poetry to international audiences around the world, most recently in Mexico City, Trinidad & Tobago, Littfest, Sweden and at University of California, Davis and Emory College in the US.

Her poems are published widely – they have been translated into Spanish, Turkish and Swedish, dropped from a helicopter over the Houses of Parliament, exhibited on Poems on the Underground, broadcast on BBC TV and Radio (BBC News 24, Radios 3 and 4) and commissioned as a dance/poetry/film collaboration.

Karen teaches creative writing at all levels, from bachelors and masters degrees (Royal Holloway, University of London) to beginners and intermediates at The Faber Academy, Arvon Foundation and The Poetry School.

Her second collection, *Seasonal Disturbances,* is published by Carcanet (2017). ■

■ MENTOR BIOGRAPHIES:

Mona Arshi *(mentor to Ian Humphreys)*
Mona Arshi was born in 1970 to Punjabi Sikh parents in West London and grew up in Hounslow. She worked for a decade as a lawyer for the human rights charity Liberty UK, acting on many high-profile cases, including that of the 'right-to-die' campaigner, Diane Pretty. Her debut collection, *Small Hands* (Liverpool University Press, 2015), awarded the Forward Prize for Best First Collection, was six years in the writing. It features poems in terza rima, ghazals and a ballad, and the subjects include the loss of her younger brother, who died three years ago. 'Observing the anguish of a family trying to come to terms and survive was a difficult task, but one I felt I had to negotiate, especially if you believe that one of the functions of poetry is to make the unbearable, bearable.' She rejects the idea that poets are overly sensitive and that poetry can only be appreciated by certain people. 'It's simply not true. Writers, and poets in particular, are pathologically inquisitive about the physical world around them and poetry is simply the world we live in, translated into language.' She studied for a Masters in Creative Writing at the University of East Anglia in 2010, won the inaugural *Magma* Poetry Competition in 2011 and was joint winner in 2014 of the Manchester Poetry Prize. Her work is included in *Ten: the new wave* (Bloodaxe Books/The Complete Works, 2014). www.monaarshi.com/

Liz Berry *(mentor to Degna Stone)*
Liz Berry was born in the Black Country and now lives in Birmingham. Her pamphlet, *The Patron Saint of Schoolgirls*, was published by Tall Lighthouse in 2010. Liz's debut collection, *Black Country* (Chatto & Windus, 2014), was a Poetry Book Society Recommendation, received a Somerset Maugham

Award, won the Geoffrey Faber Memorial Award and won the Forward Prize for Best First Collection 2014. *Black Country* was chosen as a book of the year by the *Guardian, Telegraph, Mail, Big Issue* and *Morning Star*. Liz's poems have been broadcast on BBC Radio, television and recorded for the Poetry Archive. She has been a judge for major prizes including the Forward Prizes and Foyle Young Poets, and works as a tutor for the Arvon Foundation, Writers' Centre Norwich and Writing West Midlands.

Catherine Smith *(mentor to Victoria Adukwei Bulley)*
Catherine Smith's first short poetry collection, *The New Bride* (Smith/Doorstop) was shortlisted for the Forward Prize for Best First Collection, 2001. Her first full-length collection, *The Butcher's Hands* (Smith/Doorstop), was a Poetry Book Society Recommendation and was shortlisted for the Aldeburgh/Jerwood Prize, 2004. In 2004 she was voted one of Mslexia's 'Top Ten UK Women Poets' and one of 'the twenty most exhilarating poets of her generation' in the PBS Next Generation Poets promotion. *Lip* (Smith/Doorstop) was shortlisted for the Forward Prize for Best Collection in 2008. Her latest full-length poetry collection is *Otherwhere* (Smith|Doorstop). Her poetry is widely anthologised – *Being Alive* (Bloodaxe), *Identity Parade* (Bloodaxe) and *The Poetry of Sex*, ed. Sophie Hannah (Penguin). She also writes short fiction and radio drama and teaches for the Creative Writing Programme in Brighton, The Poetry School and the Arvon Foundation.

Her first short fiction collection, *The Biting Point*, was published by Speechbubble Books in 2010. Her radio drama, short fiction and poetry have been broadcast by BBC Radio. In 2009 she was commissioned by the BBC to write 15 'micro-fictions' set in Oxford, for 'Made in England.' She has twice worked with Lewes Live Literature. In 2010/11 three of her short stories were adapted for a Live Literature stage performance, *Weight*, performed to critical acclaim in Brighton, Reading and Lewes. *The New Cockaigne*, a pamphlet-length supernatural, satirical poem, imagining the medieval fantasy land of Cockaigne imposed by law on 21st-century Britain (The Frogmore Press), was adapted and performed as a Live Literature show in 2014. She is currently working on some new poems, a novel and a radio drama script. www.catherinesmithwriter.co.uk

W.N. Herbert *(mentor to Yomi Sode)*
W.N. Herbert was born in Dundee, and educated at Brasenose College, Oxford, where he published his DPhil thesis (*To Circumjack MacDiarmid*, OUP, 1992). He is Professor of Poetry and Creative Writing at Newcastle University. He has published seven volumes of poetry and four pamphlets, and is widely anthologised. He has published broadly in the field of Creative Writing, and is a regular reviewer of contemporary poetry. His last six collections, with Bloodaxe Books, have won numerous accolades. He has been shortlisted twice for the T.S. Eliot Prize and twice for the Saltire. He has gained four Poetry Book Society Recommendations, and won three Scottish Arts Council Awards. In 2013 he was appointed Dundee's Makar, or city laureate. In 2014 he was received a Cholmondeley Award for his poetry, and an honorary doctorate from Dundee University. In 2015 he became a Fellow of the Royal Society of Literature.

Sarah Howe *(mentor to Will Harris)*
Sarah Howe is a British poet, academic and editor. Her first book, *Loop of Jade* (Chatto & Windus, 2015), won the T.S. Eliot Prize and the *Sunday Times* / PFD Young Writer of the Year Award, and was shortlisted for the Seamus Heaney Centre Poetry Prize and the Forward Prize for Best First Collection. Born in Hong Kong in 1983 to an English father and Chinese mother, she

moved to England as a child. Her pamphlet, *A Certain Chinese Encyclopedia* (Tall Lighthouse, 2009), won an Eric Gregory Award from the Society of Authors. She is the founding editor of *Prac Crit*, an online journal of poetry and criticism. She is currently a Leverhulme Fellow in English at University College London. www.radcliffe.harvard.edu/people/sarah-howe.

Mimi Khalvati *(mentor to Jennifer Lee Tsai)*
Mimi Khalvati was born in Tehran, Iran. She grew up on the Isle of Wight, where she attended boarding school from the age of six, and has lived most of her life in England. She trained at Drama Centre London and has worked as an actor and director in the UK and Iran. She has published eight collections of poetry with Carcanet Press, including *The Weather Wheel, The Meanest Flower*, a Poetry Book Society Recommendation, a Financial Times Book of the Year, and shortlisted for the T.S. Eliot Prize and, most recently, *Child: New and Selected Poems 1991-2011*, a Poetry Book Society Special Commendation. Her work has been translated into nine languages and she received a Cholmondeley Award in 2006. She is a Fellow of the Royal Society of Literature. Mimi is the founder of The Poetry School and was its Coordinator from 1997 to 2004. She is a core tutor for the School and has co-edited its three anthologies of new writing published by Enitharmon Press. She is also a freelance poetry tutor and has worked with arts organisations such as the Arvon Foundation and the Southbank Centre and has taught at universities in the UK, Europe and America.

Her mentoring with Jennifer Lee Tsai began in January 2017, but Karen McCarthy Woolf edited Jennifer's work for this anthology.

Hannah Lowe *(mentor to Raymond Antrobus)*
Hannah Lowe's first poetry collection, *Chick* (Bloodaxe Books,

2013), won the Michael Murphy Memorial Award for Best First Collection and was shortlisted for the Forward, Aldeburgh and Seamus Heaney first collection prizes, and was selected for the Poetry Book Society's Next Generation Poets 2014 promotion. This was followed by two pamphlets, *R x* (sine wave peak, 2013) and *Ormonde* (Hercules Editions, 2014), and her family memoir, *Long Time No See* (Periscope, 2015). Her second full-length collection, *Chan*, was published by Bloodaxe in 2016.

Pascale Petit *(mentor to Omikemi Natacha Bryan and Momtaza Mehri)*
Pascale Petit's seventh collection, *Mama Amazonica* (Bloodaxe Books, 2017), is a Poetry Book Society Choice. Her sixth, *Fauverie*, was her fourth to be shortlisted for the T.S. Eliot Prize and five poems from the book won the 2013 Manchester Poetry Prize. Petit has had three collections chosen as Books of the Year in the *Times Literary Supplement*, *Independent* and *Observer*. She received a Cholmondeley Award in 2015. Her books have been translated into Spanish (in Mexico), Chinese, French and Serbian and she is widely travelled, including in the Peruvian and Venezuelan Amazon. She is the Jerwood/Arvon mentor for poetry in 2017/18.

Michael Schmidt *(mentor to Leonardo Boix)*
Michael Schmidt is the editorial and managing director of Carcanet Press and the editor of *PN Review*. He is a literary historian, critic, translator and poet and has taught poetry at Manchester and Glasgow.

ACKNOWLEDGEMENTS

The poems in this anthology were first published here, except for the following:

Raymond Antrobus: 'Echo' was published in *Poetry*, 'To Sweeten Bitter' in *The Rialto*, and 'Jamaican British' by Goldsmiths, University of London (Poetic Diasporas exhibition).

Omikemi Natacha Bryan: the final section of 'Crownsville' was published in *Lighthouse Journal* (Issue 12, Spring 2016) and 'Salt' in *The Rialto* (87, Autumn 2016). The first five poems in her selection were included in her pamphlet, *If I talked everything my eyes saw*, (Gatehouse Press, 2016).

Victoria Adukwei Bulley: a version of 'Girls in Arpeggio' was published in the Barbican Young Poets anthology of 2014-15, and appears in her pamphlet Girl B (African Poetry Book Fund, University of Nebraska Press, 2017) with 'Retreat'. 'Lost Belonging' was broadcast on BBC Radio 4 in Glyn Maxwell's *How to Write a Poem* (August 2016). A version of 'Why can't a K be beautiful and magic?' features on *Badilisha Poetry X-change*, an online archive for Pan-African poetry from across the world (www.badilishapoetry.com)

Will Harris: 'Self-portrait in front of a small mirror' was published in *The Rialto* (Issue 86), 'Mother's Country' in *The Rialto* (Issue 87), and 'Halo 2' in *The Poetry Review* (106:4).

Momtaza Mehri: 'I believe in the transformative power of breakfast cereal and cocoa butter' appeared in *Puerto Del Sol* (April 2016), '<p>Grief in HTML</p>' in *Public Pool*, (August 2016), 'Dis-rupture' as a sound piece in *Buzzfeed*, https://www.buzzfeed.com/aishagani/somali-nation-of-poets?utm_term=.

qqMRaM5Ox#.kqZpqk2jn, June 2016) and then in *PANK* (Fall/ Winter 2016 Issue), and 'The unthought has a comb' in *The Rialto* (Issue 87, Autumn 2016).

Yomi Sode: 'The Outing' first appeared in The Rialto (87, Autumn 2016) and 'Night Terrors' and 'Wón Ti Dé' in *Bare Lit* anthology (March 2017).

Degna Stone: 'The River Gods' was published in the inaugural issue of *Lucifer Magazine* (2016). The third poem from the 'A Lick of Me Shoe' sequence was published in *Urban Myths and Legends* (The Emma Press, 2016). The definition of Sub-acute Bacterial Endocarditis is taken from the Health Central website. The epigraph from 'Cross Bones Burial Ground' is taken from 'Black Ice and Rain' by Michael Donaghy.

Jennifer Lee Tsai: 'The Valley Spirit Never Dies' was published in *Smoke* (62).

Author photographs: Kariima Ali (Momtaza Mehri), Caleb Femi (Leonardo Boix, Yomi Sode), Suzanne Lau (Jennifer Lee Tsai), Joao Leal (Omikemi Natacha Bryan), Fiona Melville (Karen McCarthy Woolf), Jolade Olusanya (Yomi Sode), Timothy Pulford-Cutting (Victoria Ann Bulley), Daniel Stone (Degna Stone), Jem Talbot (Will Harris), Sarah Turton (Ian Humphreys), Naomi Woddis (Raymond Antrobus).